The 21st Century Elementary Library Media Program

The 21st Century Elementary Library Media Program

Carl A. Harvey II

A LINWORTH PUBLISHING BOOK

LIBRARIES UNLIMITED
An Imprint of ABC-CLIO, LLC

A B C ⬧ C L I O

Santa Barbara, California • Denver, Colorado • Oxford, England

Library of Congress Cataloging-in-Publication Data

Harvey, Carl A.
    The 21st century elementary library media program / Carl A. Harvey.
        p. cm.
    Includes bibliographical references and index.
    ISBN 978-1-58683-381-7 (acid-free paper)
    1. Elementary school libraries—United States.   2. Instructional materials
centers—United States.   I. Title.   II. Title: Twenty-first century elementary
library program.
    Z675.S3H2687   2010
    027.8'2220973—dc22   2009041722

14   13   12   11   10   1   2   3   4   5

This book is also available on the World Wide Web as an eBook.
Visit www.abc-clio.com for details.

ABC-CLIO, LLC
130 Cremona Drive, P.O. Box 1911
Santa Barbara, California 93116-1911

This book is printed on acid-free paper (∞)

Manufactured in the United States of America

Core Beliefs are excerpted from Standards for the 21st-Century Learner by the American Association of School
Librarians, a division of the American Library Association, copyright © 2007 American Library Association.
AASL's *Standards for the 21st Century Learner.* Used with permission.

Contents

Acknowledgments

Thanks, as always, to my amazing family. Their support of each new project and endeavor has always been unwavering!

Thanks to the Linworth family—Marlene, Cyndee, Kate, and everyone who helped guide this book along to publication—I want to say, a huge thank you! Your constant support and guidance has been a real blessing!

This book is dedicated to the students and faculty at North Elementary School. In 2002, I walked through the halls of North as part of the interview for their library media specialist position and instantly felt the vibe of the building. The culture at North is truly one of a great big family. I knew it was a place I wanted to be. The library media program, like everything at North, is a team effort. Without teachers willing to collaboratively plan, teach, and assess; without administrators who support and encourage; without students who love their library media center; and without parents who support the program, we would not have been able to create our successful library media program! While we are thrilled with what we have been able to achieve, we are always looking for what will help us take it up to that next level. I thank the teachers, administrators, students, and parents for their trust and belief that by working together we could create amazing learning experiences for our students through the library media program.

Figures

About the Author

CARL A. HARVEY II is the library media specialist at North Elementary School in Noblesville, Indiana. In his school he serves as cochair of the School Improvement Committee and chair of the Media/Tech Advisory Committee. He is active in many professional organizations including: the Association for Indiana Media Educators (AIME), having served as president, conference chair, Young Hoosier Book Award general chair, and survivor workshop chair; the Indiana Library Federation (ILF), having served as president and conference chair; and the American Association of School Librarians (AASL), having served as chair of the Affiliate Assembly, cochair of the 2007 AASL Conference, and currently a member-at-large on the AASL Board of Directors. He has published articles in various professional journals, and has written two books—*The Library Media Specialist in the Writing Process* (coauthored with Marge Cox and Susan Page) (2007) and *No School Library Left Behind: Leadership, School Improvement, and the Media Specialist* (2008), published by Linworth Publishing. Carl has presented at numerous state and national conferences, and is a member of several advisory boards. Some of his awards include Outstanding New Library Media Specialist (1999), Outstanding Media Specialist (2007) and the Peggy L. Pfeiffer Service Award (2007) from the Association for Indiana Media Educators. The library media program at North Elementary School has been recognized with the Blue Ribbon for Exemplary School Media Programs in Indiana (2005) and the National School Library Media Program of the Year Award (2007). Carl also consults part time for C.L.A.S.S. (Connected Learning Assures Successful Students) in Indianapolis, Indiana.

Introduction

Excitement and opportunities abound for today's library media programs. The rapid expansion of information available in a multitude of formats has created not only an abundance of resources but also the need for skills to find, evaluate, and use that information effectively. The explosion of Web 2.0 and the open source tools and resources available have increased the ability for students to be a part of creating and disseminating new information. Library media programs are a critical link to preparing students for this new environment.

In 2007, the American Association of School Librarians released the *Standards for the 21st Century Learner,* the International Society for Technology Educators released the next generation of the *National Educational Technology Standards (NETS),* and the Partnership for the 21st Century release their *Framework for 21st Century Learning.* These documents paint a picture of the skills students need to be successful. Library media instruction has focused on inquiry and helping guide students to find, evaluate, and use information accurately and effectively. Articulated in a new format that embraces the changes in the information and technology landscape, these standards make it even more apparent that library media programs are a critical link to preparing students for this new environment.

The new environment requires library media specialists to rethink and reform the elementary library media program. Just as the skills students need for the 21st century are changing, ways that students learn are changing. Library media specialists need to ride the wave of this change and redefine their programs in order to ensure that students are successful in the 21st century. This moment in time provides an opportunity to reshape what the library media specialist does and in turn helps paint a new image. Library media specialists are uniquely positioned to take the lead in 21st-century skills. It is time to get ready for the adventures that lie ahead by redefining the role library media programs play in today's (and tomorrow's) elementary schools.

In the pages that follow, there is a plethora of ideas and strategies for creating, implementing, and managing an elementary library media center. As one reads these pages, new information and new tools to share that information are being created. Keeping up with and harnessing the best of all that information and tools for student learning will be the job of the 21st century library media specialist!

In Chapter 1, the focus is on the role of the library media program in the past, the present, and the future. The role library media programs have played in schools has been changing and evolving for years. How does the 21st-century environment continue to change that role? Chapter 2 focuses on the people library media specialists work with every day. How does the library media specialist work with various stakeholders? Why are they important? What opportunities for partnership and collaboration are available? Chapter 3 focuses on communication. Library media specialists must be effective communicators so that stakeholders know what they do, how and why they do it, how they can help, and why the media specialist's role in the school is so vital.

Chapter 4 focuses on curriculum. The heart of the library media program is the connection made between 21st-century standards and the classroom curriculum. How do library media specialist and teachers collaborate? How does the library media specialist make those connections with teachers? What role does the library media specialist play in assessment? Chapter 5 is all about the programming offered to students. Beyond instruction, what kind of programming should the library media specialist create to promote reading, provide enrichment programs, host celebrations, and so forth? What events bring the students into the library media center? Chapter 6 focuses on technology. How does technology affect the library media center? While a separate chapter focuses on technology, technology is embedded into all the chapters because that is the reality of the 21st century.

Chapter 7 looks at library administration. Behind-the-scenes jobs have to be done to make the library media program function effectively. How can some of the new Web tools out there make the library media specialist's job easier? Chapter 8 examines budgets. Money certainly doesn't grow on trees, so how does the library media specialist find money to support the program? What are some alternatives to funding provided by the school? Chapter 9 talks about library collections and the influx of new formats of materials. How do 21st-century students' needs and interests change what library media centers collections look like? How does technology affect the collection?

The book concludes with two more chapters. Chapter 10 focuses on advocacy. It is important for the library media specialist to get past being the sole advocate for the library media program. How does the library media specialist motivate and enlist others to go out there and be the voice for the program? Chapter 11 is all about the library media specialist's role as a leader. There is no doubt that successful library media specialists are leaders in their schools. Why is that important? How does being involved beyond the library media center help promote the library media program?

Finally, each chapter ends with a Wiki-Wrap Up. This provides a place to wrap up each chapter but also provides a way to continue the conversation. A companion wiki to this book has been posted online at http://www.carl-harvey.com/librarytieswiki. The wiki will have links to additional examples and resources.

The author's intent for the pages that follow is to provide ideas, strategies, and tips that can help the library media program to continue to develop and grow. The library media specialist should never be content with the status quo, but rather should be constantly looking for opportunities and experiences that will take the library media program to the next level. Whether the reader is just starting out in the library media center or is a seasoned veteran, the key is to look ahead so that the library media program evolves as the needs of the students and staff evolves. One thing that hasn't changed is that library media programs of the 21st century will continue to develop and foster a culture of life-long learning for everyone.

CHAPTER 1

The Elementary Library Media Program—Past, Present, and Future

As good as we are, we can always get better.

—Barbara Pedersen, President and Founder, C.L.A.S.S.
(Connected Learning Assures Successful Students)

In every workshop she gives, every meeting she runs, every aspect of the business she operates, and in every classroom she works in, Barbara shares her vision for moving forward. It has become a personal mantra for many. What a powerful message to celebrate the current realities but at the same time focus thoughts on what can be done next to make it even better! Much of this book will focus on taking those next steps to get even better.

Elementary library media programs have been getting better for years. From nonexistent, to a place where students checked out resources, to a place where students are finding, evaluating, using, and creating information, elementary library media programs have continued to evolve and grow. Programs will continue to alter in the 21st century. As the needs of students and learning environments change, so will the library media program.

The Past

The history of elementary school libraries is brief. Libraries in schools were just beginning as the 20th century began. Most of those libraries were also in secondary schools. The following timeline lists some of the major events in the history of elementary school libraries and how they have changed over the years.

Mid-1800s to 1900	Schools are beginning to put collections together in libraries in the late 1800s. The first school librarians are hired right around the turn of the century. Most of these libraries and librarians are at secondary level schools (Woolls 11).
1896	The National Education Association (NEA) creates a School Library Section (Morris 4).
1914	The American Library Association (ALA) creates a School Library Section (Morris 4).
1920	The first school library standards are published by ALA. *Standard Library Organization and Equipment for Secondary Schools* is written by a committee under the chairmanship of Charles C. Certain. While these standards do not mention or apply to elementary school, the conversation begins about what school libraries in the United States should look like (Morris 7).
1925	The ALA and the NEA publish the first standards for elementary school libraries—also chaired by Charles C. Certain. However, not many elementary schools have libraries, and the books that are published are often part of collections in the classroom (Woolls 10, Morris 8).
1945	*School Libraries for Today and Tomorrow* is published by ALA. These standards paint a picture of the different roles between public librarians and school librarians. Frances Henne, a member of the committee who wrote the 1945 standards, advocates for collaboration between school librarians and classroom teachers (Kester and Jones 954).
1951	AASL is formed as a division of ALA.
1960	*Standards for School Library Programs* is published by AASL. Nineteen other professional organizations cooperate on this project. These standards highlight the school librarian's role as a teacher and begin to articulate the incorporation of audio-visual materials in school libraries (Kester and Jones 956).
1964	U.S. Office of Education report by Mary Helen Mahar and Doris C. Holladay says that fewer than 50 percent of elementary schools have libraries (Woolls 13).
1965	The Elementary and Secondary Education Act (ESEA) is passed, including funds specifically to purchase school library materials (Title II).
1969	AASL and NEA's Department of Audiovisual Instruction (DAVI) publish *Standards for School Media Programs*. These guidelines provide detailed quantitative guidelines for school libraries (Kester and Jones 958).

1975	AASL and Association for Educational Communications and Technology (formerly DAVI) publish *Media Programs: District and School* (Kester and Jones 959). These standards begin to place a greater emphasis on the instructional role of the library media specialist.
1979	The first White House Conference on Library and Information Science is held in Washington, DC. They make 64 recommendations, including a guarantee of media services in each public school. Unfortunately, cuts in government spending in the 1980s delay the implementation of the recommendations (Morris 15).
1980s	Funding requirements are rewritten and school libraries are required to compete for funds both at the federal and state level. Changes in certification have been altered so that in some places a certified library media specialist is not required in the school library (Woolls 14).
1988	*Information Power* is published jointly by the AASL and the Association for Educational Communications and Technology. The new standards focus on the role of the library media specialist as a teacher, information specialist, and instructional consultant.
1990s	There is rapid growth of technology in school libraries during the 1990s. Most become automated and connected to the Internet. Back-Rub (which was renamed Google) is developed in January 1996. Blogging begins around 1997.
1998	*Information Power: Building Partnerships for Learning* is published by the AASL and the Association for Educational Communications and Technology. This document added to the role of the library media specialist as program administrator and instructional partner. The document also includes the *Information Literacy Standards for Student Learning*.

The Present

First Lady Laura Bush hosted the White House Conference on School Libraries on June 4, 2002. In her opening remarks, Mrs. Bush said, "Libraries allow children to ask questions about the world and find the answers. And the wonderful thing is that once a child learns to use a library, the doors to learning are always open" (Bush). Many current leaders such as Dr. Gary Hartzell and Dr. Keith Curry Lance spoke at the conference and shared the importance of school libraries in today's schools (Morris 18–19).

But that door is a little different now. The way students learn, the tools they have access to, and the way library media specialists and teachers educate them is all changing. The technology elements continue to explode. Web 2.0 has changed the Internet by making it interactive and social with Web sites such as Wikipedia in 2001; Second Life in 2003; Flickr, Facebook, and Delicious in 2004; and Twitter in 2006. All of these new formats are forcing educators to think about how and what students learn.

In 2007, the AASL released the *Standards for 21st Century Learner* (http://www.ala.org/ala/mgrps/divs/aasl/guidelinesandstandards/learningstandards/standards.cfm). The new standards focus on inquiry, social learning, and ethical skills and are designed to provide a framework of skills students will need for the future. Library media specialists will take these to work with classroom teachers as they combine them with content area standards to design lessons and units.

At the same time, the International Society for Technology in Education (ISTE) released their refresh of the *National Educational Technology Standards for Students* (NETS; http://www.iste.org/AM/Template.cfm?Section=NETS). The original NETS focused on the technology tools that students needed to learn, but the revised version centers on the skills they will need to live in a digital society.

There are some areas that overlap in both sets of standards. For example, information literacy is a huge component in each document. Doug Johnson on his Blue Skunk blog created an Inspiration file comparing the *Standards for 21st Century Learner* and the NETS (http://doug-johnson.squarespace.com/blue-skunk-blog/2008/1/7/student-standard-comparisons-and-a-clean-garage.html). This visual helps to see where the writers of these standards had some commonalities.

In January 2009, AASL released *The Standards for the 21st Century Learner in Action.* This new document took the standards and provided examples and benchmarks at various levels along with potential assessment options. It helped to paint a picture for what the new standards looked like at elementary, middle, and high school.

In the spring of 2009, the AASL released the long-awaited guidelines that would replace *Information Power 2.* The new guidelines were titled *Empowering Learners: Guidelines for School Library Media Program* (http://www.ala.org/ala/mgrps/divs/aasl/guidelinesandstandards/learningstandards/guidelines.cfm). The new document divides the guidelines into three sections—"Teaching for Learning," "Building the Learning Environment," and "Empowering Learning through Leadership." The new guidelines complement the previous two versions released by AASL and complete a package of resources that paint the picture of the 21st-century library media center. AASL has also developed an implementation program called Learning 4 Life (L4L) (http://www.ala.org/ala/mgrps/divs/aasl/guidelinesandstandards/learning4life/index.cfm) to help promote and educate the world about these new resources.

The last major document that also has implications for school libraries of the future is the *Framework from the Partnership for 21st Century Skills*, released in 2007. The Partnership for 21st Century Skills (P21) made up of mostly business-related companies has outlined what they believe students in the 21st century (http://www.21stcenturyskills.org/index.php?Itemid=120&id=254&option=com_content&task=view) will need to be successful. AASL is a member of the Partnership, and many states are signing on to this initiative. A few of the components included in the P21 framework of student outputs are information, media, and technology skills, which is a place where the library media program can have an impact.

The Future

The future depends on today's library media specialists. Taking the documents from AASL, ISTE, and the Partnership for the 21st Century Skills as guides, library media specialists have the opportunity to develop a library media program that is essential for today's (and tomorrow's) students. We can be the leaders in our library media centers, in our schools, and in our districts for designing curriculum and instruction that will help prepare our students for the 21st century. By doing so, we demonstrate the essential role we play in the education environment.

In the *Standards for the 21st Century Learners,* AASL articulates these common beliefs:

✦ Reading is a window to the world.

✦ Inquiry provides a framework for learning.

✦ Ethical behavior in the use of information must be taught.

✦ Technology skills are crucial for future employment needs.

✦ Equitable access is a key component for education.

✦ The definition of information literacy has become more complex as resources and technologies have changed.

✦ The continuing expansion of information demands that all individuals acquire the thinking skills that will enable them to learn on their own.

✦ Learning has a social context.

✦ School libraries are essential to the development of learning skills (American Association of School Librarians).

Each of these common beliefs is reflected both in the *Standards for the 21st Century Learner* and in the *Empowering Learners: Guidelines for School Library Media Programs.* They are the heart of what we believe as a profession. The final belief says it all—school libraries are *essential.* The future of school libraries will be dependent on building a program around these common beliefs and in turn creating a climate where everyone in the building—not just the library media specialist—holds these common beliefs.

Wiki Wrap-Up

This is an exciting time to be a library media specialist. There is great potential in what the future holds. Library media specialists have to be ready to take that opportunity and lead! The key to the future is the library media specialists who, building on the standards and guidelines, have great potential to be change agents in their schools. For additional resources, check out the companion wiki website (http://www.carl-harvey.com/librarytieswiki/).

Works Cited

American Association of School Librarians. *Empowering Learners: Guidelines for School Library Media Programs.* Chicago: American Association of School Librarians, 2009.

American Association of School Librarians. *Standards for the 21st Century Learner.* Chicago: American Association of School Librarians, 2007.

American Association of School Librarians. *Standards for the 21st Century Learner in Action*. Chicago: American Association of School Librarians, 2009.

Bush, Laura. "Opening Remarks." White House Conference on School Libraries. White House, Washington, DC, June 4, 2002, http://www.whitehouse.gov/news/releases/2002/06/20020604-12.html.

International Society for Technology in Education. *National Educational Technology Standards for Students* (2nd ed.). Eugene, OR: International Society for Technology in Education, 2007.

Kester, Diane D. and Plummer Alton Jones. "Frances Henne and the Development of School Library Standards." *Library Trends* 52 (Spring 2004): 952–62.

Morris, Betty J. *Administering the School Library Media Center* (4th ed.). Westport, CT: Libraries Unlimited, 2004.

The Partnership for 21st Century Skills. "The Partnership for 21st Century Skills—Framework for 21st Century Learning." May 9, 2009, http://www.21stcenturyskills.org/index.php?option=com_content&task=view&id=254&Itemid=120.

Woolls, Blanche. *The School Library Manager* (3rd ed.). Westport, CT: Libraries Unlimited, 2004.

CHAPTER 2

People

Influence is derived from the perceptions of the person to be influenced, not from the perceptions of the person doing the influencing. The key to building influence lies in your ability to shape the perceptions of others.

—Dr. Gary Hartzell, from *Building Influence for the School Librarian: Tenets, Targets, and Tactics* (2nd ed.)

The biggest part of the library media specialist's job is working with people—teachers, students, parents, principals, school boards, community members, volunteers, and other library media specialists. All of these groups have a very important impact on library media specialists but at a variety of different levels. Hartzell divides two such levels—level 1 contains administrators, principals, and school board members, and level 2 contains students, parents, and community members (Hartzell 91). Level 1 has direct control over the resources needed. Level 2 does not but can be important because the ability to influence that group can affect and influence the decision made by level 1. Determining the needs of each group gives the library media specialist the opportunity not only to meet those needs but also to exceed them. Each group has a perception of the library media specialist, so it is important to either confirm they are correct or clear up any misconceptions they might have about library media programs and the role of the library media specialist.

When starting out as a library media specialist or even just switching to a new school, one of the very first things a library media specialist must do is build relationships. Everything in the library media program is dependent on the relationships built with stakeholders, so the key in the beginning is to build those bridges. Often it is easy to get caught up in fixing things in the library media center (the fiction section needs to be shifted, or the nonfiction collection needs to be weeded), but those things can wait. The most important element is building a strong solid working relationship!

The Library Media Specialist Works With Principals

Most administrators only learn about library media programs from one source—library media specialists! A recent study in Indiana showed that over 90 percent of principals learned about library media programs from their on-the-job interactions with their library media specialist (Lance, Rodney, and Russell 65). They know about the experiences they had as a child in school, as a teacher in a school, and now as an administrator in a school. Take advantage of that opportunity to help guide them on their journey of learning about the value, potential, and power of the library media program (see Figure 2.1).

Conversations with an administrator often include some of these phrases:

✦ My budget is inadequate.

✦ My support staff is insufficient.

✦ My technology is all out of date.

✦ I don't have any time for the administrative functions of the library.

This type of conversation can quickly turn off administrators. At the same time, such statements may reflect the reality of the library media specialist's situation. However, phrasing is the key. Consider these revised statements:

✦ With the new initiative for math, I've been reviewing the math collection. Most of the titles are out of date. The average copyright date is 1976. To support the projects teachers are assigning and to provide the resources students need to succeed, additional funds are needed.

✦ Yesterday two classes were in the library media center working on research, but the computers wouldn't connect to the databases because they were too slow. It wasted an hour of instructional time for that class. Do you think we could write a grant to update our computers?

✦ During the last three weeks, I have been booked solid with classes. At the same time, a tremendous amount of books circulated from the library, and the new books that I selected and ordered are still sitting in the boxes. How can teaching and learning be the focus but at the same time allow time to complete these clerical jobs? The overflowing cart of books is important because no one has had any time to shelve them so students can read them again. Could you help me find some volunteers for the library?

These statements contain the same information as the previous statements, but the difference is that the latter statements connected it directly to student learning and achievement. The second set of statements contained data as well to support the argument. Now, this does not mean that changing the phrases will automatically change the answer a library media specialist might receive from an administrator. However, it may just leave a seed planted in the administrator's mind if additional resources do become available.

A library media specialist is a teacher.   They work with students in the library media center, the computer lab, and the classroom. They teach student how to be information literate.

A library media specialist is a collaborator.   They work with teachers to plan, instruct, and evaluate student learning. They work with administrators to implement building-wide initiatives and the school improvement plan.

A library media specialist is a resource locator.   They help you find answers to questions and help find resources (all kinds) to support instruction and make informed decisions.

A library media specialist is a communicator.   They should be talking, emailing, sharing, and so forth with administrators, teachers, students, parents, and community members. They should be talking about how the library media program directly relates to the vision of the school.

A library media specialist is a leader.   Administrators and teachers see them as a leader. They are active on school committees, contribute to building initiatives, and are respected for their thoughts and ideas.

A library media specialist is a professional development provider.   They design and present professional development that supports the school improvement plan.

A library media specialist is an innovator.   They are willing to try new things. They are looking for new ways to get even better. They are creative to work around obstacles.

A library media specialist has a global perspective.   They work with everyone in the school, so they can see the entire building dynamics.

A library media specialist loves to learn.   They love to learn about new ideas and strategies for working with students and teachers. They want to be lifelong learners just like they hope their students will be.

A library media specialist is a technology integrator.   They are a leader in using technology in their instruction. They work to help administrators see how technology can be used effectively and guide purchasing decisions.

But most of all, the library media specialist does not work alone.   For a school to have a successful library media program it takes everyone (the library media specialist, teachers, administrators, and the library media staff) working together for the benefit of the students.

Figure 2.1   What should an administrator expect a school library media specialist to be?

Originally published in *Library Media Connection,* October 2009.

Library media specialists and administrators have more in common than one might think.

- ✦ The principal and library media specialist work with every staff member.

- ✦ The principal and library media specialist interact with all students.

- ✦ The principal and library media specialist need to be curriculum leaders in the school.

- ✦ The principal and library media specialist have administrative roles such as dealing with budgets, facilities, and so forth.

- ✦ The principal and library media specialist have a global perspective, being able to see the big picture of what is happening in the school.

- ✦ The principal and library media specialist (especially in elementary school) have a job where they are the only one in their building.

These similarities can lead to the opportunity for the two to share in conversations that no one else in the building could have. Many administrators come to rely on their library media specialist because they can talk about school improvement, issues in the building, and so forth with them because the library media specialist can see beyond just the classroom or grade level. Library media specialists will find they build influence by connecting these similarities between a principal and library media specialist role in the school (Hartzell 31).

An administrator is just another patron in your library media center, but just like all the other groups, their needs are different. They are looking for ways to move the school forward. How do they improve student achievement? How do they provide professional development? How do they implement instructional strategies? The library media specialists should be following what the administrator is thinking and doing. Just as with other patrons, providing them with resources, ideas, and support will garner a positive reaction.

Consider the principal who is implementing a new instructional model for the school. Should the library media specialist look for ways to implement that in their instruction? Yes! During collaborative planning sessions, could the library media specialist support and suggest ways teachers could implement the new model? Yes! Could the library media specialist provide training and ideas such as how to use technology with the new model? Yes! Administrators will notice what is happening, but you should use some of the communication tools discussed in Chapter 3 to make sure they know what is going on.

Words only go so far. Actions speak louder. Look for ways to demonstrate the program you want to achieve. Invite administrators down for lessons and programs. Demonstrate for them how what is happening in the library media center affects student achievement. Follow up with an e-mail thanking them for visiting and providing the administrator with ideas on how to continue to push to the next level.

The library media specialist does not always know what kind of experience his or her administrator has had with library media programs in the past. Library media specialists need to be intentional with what they do, say, write, and so forth to help paint the picture of what the 21st-century library media program looks like and why it is a critical element for student success.

Teachers

Library media specialists have a unique role in the school because they have the opportunity to work with every teacher in the building. This potential for impact is huge. Teachers are half of the equation to collaboration and instruction in the library media center. They bring with them the content standards, and library media specialists bring the skills and inquiry process. Marrying the two provides for quality learning opportunities for students.

Students are assigned a teacher for an entire year in elementary school, so to reach the students, the library media specialist has to connect with the teacher. Elementary teachers can be very protective of their students. Often the media specialist must work to develop a level of trust. Teachers have to believe that the library media specialist can teach their students just as effectively as they can. This trust takes time to develop. The library media specialist must remain patient, persistent, and follow through when making promises in order to begin to establish that trust.

When collaborating with teachers, library media specialists usually need a thick skin. Don't take it personally if teachers don't jump up and down with excitement over a proposed project or lesson. Keep throwing out the ideas and suggestions, and eventually one will connect. Persistence is important. Be aware of the standards they need to cover. Be aware of areas on the standardized tests where students struggle. Be aware of the themes and units in their curriculum. Use that knowledge to help better define a rationale for working with the library media specialist. Just like administrators, most teachers will welcome help and assistance.

The phrase "work with the living" applies when looking for collaborative partners. This is a good place to start, but it is important that library media specialists strive to work with all teachers. Library media specialists must work toward breaking down barriers, so they work with all the teachers (and therefore students) in the building (see Figure 2.2).

Ideas to break down those barriers include the following:

✦ Connect with the teacher's interest or passion. What kind of resources, projects, or ideas can the library media specialist suggest that will support and enhance student learning?

✦ Connect with the content the teacher hates. If there is a part of their curriculum they don't like teaching, this could be a perfect opportunity to suggest collaborating together. The teachers get through something they hate, and the students get a worthwhile learning experience.

✦ Be aware of standardized testing results. In what areas did the students in the building receive low scores? How could the library media program offer a project or activity that might help students improve in that area? Use that as an opening when trying to work with teachers.

✦ During staff meetings, professional development meetings, or anything working with staff members, model using the tools and resources that would be possible to use with students. Suggest that just as the library media specialist is helping the faculty, he or she would also be glad to use these same activities and resources with students as well.

A library media specialist is a teacher.   They work with students in the library media center, the computer lab, and the classroom. They help teach students how to be information literate.

A library media specialist is a collaborator.   They work with teachers to plan, instruct, and evaluate student learning.

A library media specialist is a resource locator.   They help you find answers to questions and help find resources (all kinds) to support instruction in the classroom. They may not always be able to succeed, but they always try their best.

A library media specialist loves literature.   They enjoy sharing great books with students and teachers. They help entice students to have a lifetime love of reading. They have ideas on incorporating great books into a variety of curriculum topics. Share with them the great books you find, too.

A library media specialist is technology literate.   They work with students to use technology in the library media center, the computer, and the classroom.

A library media specialist is a staff developer.   They help teachers learn new technologies and how to use them with students.

A library media specialist is an innovator.   They are quick to come up with ideas and are open to new ideas from others, too.

A library media specialist is a manager.   With the assistance of many people, the library media specialist makes sure the library media center runs effectively and efficiently.

A library media specialist lends a helping hand.   They are always willing to help out when needed even with it isn't their job. Ask for their help when needed. It makes them happy to be of service.

A library media specialist is flexible.   They are very willing to make changes when changes need to be made. Although they are planners, they are able to see that sometimes adjustments in plans are necessary.

A library media specialist loves to learn.   They love to hear about the great books people are reading and new ideas and strategies for working with students. Share with them new things you learn, too.

But most of all, the library media specialist does not work alone.   For a school to have a successful library media program, it takes everyone (the library media specialist, teachers, administration, and the library media staff) working together for the benefit of the students.

Figure 2.2   What should a teacher expect a school library media specialist to be?

Originally published in *Library Media Connection,* February 2005.

Often library media specialists are frustrated when teachers refuse to work with them. The job requires a certain level of persistence and a knack for seizing opportunities at just the right time.

In 2000, David V. Loertscher published his *Library Media Specialist's Taxonomy* (2nd ed.). In it he talked about the various levels of interaction the library media specialist had with curriculum and teachers. It began with the lowest level of no involvement, moved to gathering and sharing resources, and eventually near the top of his 10 levels came the development of the library media specialist actively engage in writing, planning, teaching, and assessing curriculum. At the top level, the library media specialist was not an afterthought but a critical component to designing instruction.

To hit the top of the taxonomy is not something that is going to happen over night but rather by the library media specialist working persistently and professionally to build relationships with teachers. The best way to build a relationship with a teacher is to deliver on your promises. Follow-through is key. This continues to build the level of trust.

Library media specialists also have to be where the teachers are! Waiting for teachers to come to the library could be a lonely wait—especially if the teachers are not used to someone dynamic in that role. Go to where the teachers are! Eat lunch in the lunchroom and vary the time as much as possible to eat with different grade levels. Attend grade level planning meetings. Participate in social events and on school-wide committees. Just positively interacting with teachers every day helps to build relationships that can lead to instructional collaborations!

While the first connections are likely made with classroom teachers, it is also important to reach out to related arts teachers (art, music, physical education, etc.), special education teachers, literacy coaches, and the school counselor. All of these folks teach kids too, so it is important to look for the collaborative potential with every teacher in the building.

School Boards

Every year in April during National School Library Media Month, a district library coordinator sends a package updating the school board about the role school libraries played in the district. Another library media specialist makes sure that for every literacy event, such as the annual author visit, an invitation is always sent to each of the school board members. Still another library media specialist has annual reading days where she invites the community—including school board members—to the library media center to read stories with students. A great way for a school board member to learn what is happening in the library media center is by bringing him or her in to see it.

Working with school boards directly will require some preplanning on behalf of the library media specialist. Any communication with the school board should go through the superintendent to ensure the proper chain of command. Consider an invitation to tour the library media center or the library media specialists in a district could make a group presentation to the school board highlighting the role they play in their schools. If the official channels are not an option, there are other ways school board members can learn about the program. Invite the local paper or media in for a positive story because of a program or project. School members will take notice. Make sure before contacting the media to follow any district guidelines.

Students

At the heart of the library media programs are the number one patrons—students. During the five to seven years that students are in elementary school, the library media specialist is one of the few teachers who they will work with each year. They should feel comfortable asking for help. They should feel comfortable coming to the library media center. Consider the student who, every time his class comes to check out books, heads straight for the library media specialist's office. He knows if he needs help finding a book, or has a question, or just needs a quieter place for a moment, he is always welcome to visit the library media specialist.

There are a couple of ways that library media specialists get the opportunity to connect with students. The first is during instruction. Whether this is in a collaborative planned environment or whether it is during a specials time when the library media specialist is covering prep time, either way provides the chance for the library media specialist to work with students. Another way is by creating an environment where students enjoy coming to the library media center during recess or other free time to read and explore.

Consider the reference interview between a librarian and a patron. The first part of that equation is that the person needing information has to feel comfortable and willing to go to the library media specialist and ask his or her questions. The same can be said for elementary students. They have to feel comfortable that the library media specialist is there to help them. Attitudes are important. While one is not going to give them the answer, they need to feel they have the support to help guide them to where they can find the answer.

Library collections in schools are focused heavily on curriculum but at the same time also contain resources for general student interests. Students love coming to the library to learn and explore. Consider the school where there are puppets available for students to create their own show during recess. Another school has a writing center set up with paper, crayons, pencils, and so forth that students can use to create their own writing adventures. Another library media center has a math center filled with games, problem-solving resources, and other math-related resources. Students know that any time they are in the library media center they can use any of these things. The climate is such that students feel free to explore and learn.

The library media center space is one that belongs to everyone. Students should feel that sense of being not only welcomed but also that is a place they belong. They will have great ideas to make the library even better, so make sure to take time to ask them their thoughts. Chapter 10 will talk more about advisory committees and ways to gather input from stakeholders.

Parents

Some parents' only interactions with the library media program are when they hear about lost or overdue books. Look for ways to keep parents informed of what happens in the library media center beyond just those notices. Give them the opportunity to see the positive things happening in the library media center. Write pieces for the school newsletter. Consider sending home a library media center newsletter. Instead of using paper, use e-mail or post it on the school Web page. For those students without online access, make sure to send home paper copies so every family is aware of what is happening. How about setting up a library media center blog to showcase what is happening in the library media center? The blog could serve two purposes because it would also serve as a way to communicate to students, teachers, and administrators. When working on projects that require students to spend time on them at home, send home a list of resources students can access from the school library Web site.

Solicit parent volunteers. They can be invaluable to helping return materials to the shelves, processing new materials, running book fairs, and so forth. At the same time, this gives them a prime view of what is happening in the library media center. They can see the classes and projects. They can see the benefits the program has for their child(ren).

PTA/PTO groups are another great way to share what is happening in the library media center. Attend their meetings and talk about the library media program. Consider ways that the library media specialist can support them. How about offering to update their Web page? How about volunteering to help them with enrichment programs? Thank them for supporting the library media center. They often want to support things that will benefit the entire school—the library media program is a perfect place!

Community Members

One of the major connections with the community is the partnership one can build with local business. Whenever possible, the library media specialist should look for ways to connect with local businesses. For example, ask an independent bookstore to help provide books for an author visit. Or, as part of a reading celebration incentive, take students on a field trip to the local ice cream shop and then a visit to the local independent bookstore to purchase books for the library media center.

The newspaper or library media center Web site is a great way for the community to read about the library media program. Share information about programs, projects, or even some of the great resources available. One district of library media specialists writes a weekly book review column to share with the community. When the local newspaper stopped publishing the reviews, they moved them to the district Web site for the community to continue to enjoy.

Consider having students post a podcast about the week in review at the school—highlighting, of course, some of the things happening in the library media center. How about posting a video of the morning announcements on the Web each day? Use a blog to connect with a visiting author before they visit the school. The interaction might allow the community to participate in the discussion. Consider having the author do an evening presentation and inviting the community to join in.

The community is another place to solicit volunteers. There may be some retired folks who are looking for a way to give back to the community, or there may be business professionals who have a free lunch once a week where they could donate their time. Think in terms of the jobs that need to be done and then see who might be just the right volunteer to help.

Library Media Specialists

Library media specialists can be a support network for each other. Library media specialists sometimes feel isolated because there really is no other person in the building who performs their same job. It becomes important to find other library media specialists in the district, in the state, or even in other parts of the country where the library media specialist can share situations/problems and brainstorm solutions, get new ideas, and build a network of friends.

When there are multiple library media specialists in a school district, it is great to get together once a month to talk and share. The concept is much like creating a professional learning community (PLC) of school library media specialists. According to the All Things PLC Web site (http://www.allthingsplc.info/about/aboutPLC.php), a PLC is a group of educators working together to improve student achievement. They focus on student learning, research best practices and implement them, and base all their decisions on results. District-wide coordinators will often take on the roll to make sure that happens, but in districts without a coordinator, consider starting a group in the district. Perhaps start out with a professional book to get the conversation started (see Figure 2.3 for a list of professional book study recommendations). Set protocols before starting, so that the gatherings are productive. For example:

✦ Conversations will stay positive.

✦ There is no whining.

✦ Work toward solutions.

When there is only one library media specialist in a district, it is important to branch out. Make contacts with other library media specialists in the area. Perhaps a periodical gathering at a local restaurant would be a good way to begin sharing. Gather e-mail addresses for those library media specialists willing to share or discuss ideas and create an e-mail distribution list or perhaps create a wiki, blog, or other social networking tools to foster communication.

One of the best ways to meet other library media specialists is to attend the state school library association conferences. It is a great way to build a network of library media specialists from all over the state with whom you can network for advice and ideas. National conferences allow the network to expand beyond the state boundaries.

Today's 21st-century technologies allow us to communicate and share in more ways the ever imaginable before. People are just an e-mail away from all over the world. The listserv LM_Net has been connecting library media specialists online since it began in 1992. The listserv sends questions and answers to the library media specialist's inbox in droves each day or in a daily digest mode. Just searching the LM_Net archives can provide a wealth of information for the library media specialist.

Blogs provide a way to interact what other library media specialists. Commenting on blogs brings one into the conversation. (See Appendix B for a list of "Library Media/Tech Leaders Blogs.") Consider setting up an aggregator such as Google Reader or Bloglines to keep track of all your favorite blogs.

Use Web sites like Delicious or Digg to organize Web resources. Create a tag for your group so when you find a resource you think other library media specialists might be interested in you can mark it for them.

The Teacher-Librarian Ning (http://teacherlibrarian.ning.com) started by Joyce Valenza is another online playground for library media specialists. It continues to grow and expand each day. Social networks such as Facebook or Twitter are filled with library media specialists. In

Below are just some of the professional books available that would make a good book discussion. Consider the issues in the district or area that is the most critical, choose a book on that topic, and discuss how the library media center can make an impact!

Adams, Helen. *Ensuring Intellectual Freedom and Access to Information in the School Library Media Center.* Westport, CT: Libraries Unlimited, 2008.

Anderson, Cynthia and Kathi Kopp. *Write Grants, Get Money,* (2nd ed.) Columbus, OH: Linworth Publishing, 2009.

Buzzeo, Toni. *The Collaboration Handbook.* Columbus, OH: Linworth Publishing, 2009.

Ferlazzo, Larry with Lorie Hammond. *Building Parent Engagement in Schools.* Columbus, OH: Linworth Publishing, 2009.

Harada, Violet H. and Joan M. Yoshina. *Assessing Learning: Librarians and Teachers as Partners.* Westport, CT: Libraries Unlimited, 2005.

Harvey, Carl A., II. *No School Library Left Behind: Leadership, School Improvement, and the Media Specialist.* Columbus, OH: Linworth Publishing, 2008.

Haven, Kendall. *Story Proof: The Science behind the Startling Power of Story.* Westport, CT: Libraries Unlimited, 2007.

Kuhlthau, Carol, Leslie K. Maniotes, and Ann K. Caspari. *Guided Inquiry.* Westport, CT: Libraries Unlimited, 2007.

Johnson, Mary. *Primary Source Teaching the Web 2.0 Way.* Columbus, OH: Linworth Publishing, 2009.

Jones, Jami and Alana Zambone. *The Power of the Media Specialist to Improve Academic Achievement and Strengthen At-Risk Students.* Columbus, OH: Linworth Publishing, 2007.

Richardson, Will. *Blogs, Wikis, Podcasts, and Other Powerful Web Tools for Classroom* (2nd ed.). Thousand Oaks, CA: Corwin Press, 2009.

Vande Brake, Kate, ed. *Collaborative Units That Work: TEAMS Award Winners.* Columbus, OH: Linworth Publishing, 2009.

Warlick, David. *Redefining Literacy 2.0* (2nd ed.). Columbus, OH: Linworth Publishing, 2009.

Zmuda, Allison and Violet H. Harada. *Librarians as Learning Specialists.* Westport, CT: Libraries Unlimited, 2008.

Figure 2.3 Professional book study recommendations.

the virtual world there is certainly a presence on ALA Island or International Society for Technology in Education Island in Second Life of library media specialists.

Just like no two library media programs are identical, no library media specialist is exactly like another. As colleagues interact both face-to-face and virtually, take the best and incorporate it into the library media program. Everyone can take time to learn from each other, and in the end students are the ones who benefit. David Warlick refers to the contacts one makes using technology and face-to-face interactions as creating a personal learning network (PLN). Chapter 11 describes how library media specialists can create their own PLN (Warlick).

Library Media Support Network
Support Staff

Full- or part-time assistants are a major blessing in an elementary school. Having the support of assistants to assume clerical and technical roles makes it much easier for the library media specialist to focus on the critical instructional role, working with students and teachers. Unfortunately, not every library is fortunate enough to have an assistant. The primary role of the library media specialist should be instruction and working with students and teachers. This becomes difficult when there are no assistants to help. The library media specialist will need to prioritize the various tasks and focus on the most important ones, realizing that some things just won't get done. If the books do not get back to the shelves quickly, life will go on. Maybe if people notice some things not being done, they may look for ways to help. The instructional role of the library media specialist is the most critical.

Working with assistants can sometimes be challenging—especially if the assistant was working in the library first. The best plan is to try and bring them into the planning process. Be open and let them know what is going on, why it is happening, how they can help, and how the library media specialist is going to support them. As they feel ownership in helping create and grow the program, they will work even harder to help reach the goal. Ask for their ideas and suggestions, too.

It is also a wise idea to be up front and honest. For example, if the library media specialist knows she has a control issue, share that with the assistant. If the assistant has a tendency to get overwhelmed quickly, the assistant should tell the library media specialist. The library media specialist and the assistant have to work very closely together, so it is better to communicate early on to avoid problems later.

Consider scheduling a weekly or monthly meeting with the assistant to preview the classes and projects coming up, the clerical tasks that will need to be done, and any other major events that might affect the library media center. When both sides are knowledgeable about what is going on, it creates an environment where things can get done effectively and efficiently.

Volunteers

Volunteers cannot replace paid staff, but they can help relieve some of the pressures from the library media specialist. Volunteers can shelve books, check books out, repair books, cover and process books, put up bulletin boards, organize the book fair, and perform a host of other clerical tasks, freeing up the library media specialist to work with students and instruction.

Not every volunteer can do every task. Quickly the library media specialist will discover the best match between the volunteer and the tasks. Training takes some time up front, but a good volunteer can be worth it as the year progresses. Consider asking some of the volunteers from the previous year to help train the new volunteers. Also, realize that showing them everything at once might be daunting. Pick one task, train them, and then let them work on it. The trainings can build over time as the volunteers come back. Some sources of volunteers include the following:

✦ At back-to-school nights in the fall, request a few minutes to ask for volunteers. Focus on kindergarten parents because it may be possible to find a volunteer who will stay with the library during their child's entire time at the school.

✦ Visit the PTA/PTO meeting and ask for assistance. Perhaps a parent would even take the lead in organizing the volunteer schedule.

✦ Check with senior citizen centers or other like groups where seniors are looking for ways to stay active and involved.

Remember to check your district policy for volunteers. Some districts may require a background check before allowing adults to be in contact with students. It is important to be aware of any such rules or procedures first before asking anyone to come and help.

Student Assistants

Student assistants can sometimes fill part of the void when there is a lack of volunteers or paid assistants. Students are often eager to help, and the library media center provides a variety of things students can do to help. For example:

✦ Turn on lights

✦ Turn on/shut down computers

✦ Restock the writing center with pencils, papers, and so forth

✦ Dust shelves

✦ Trim lamination

✦ Die cut letters

✦ Run copies

✦ Load paper in printers

✦ Clean computer screens

✦ Pull books for teachers

✦ Check in/check out books

✦ Straighten shelves

✦ Shelve books and other materials

This is not an all-inclusive list, but it gives an idea for a place to start. A lot depends on the students who volunteer and the level at which they can handle the tasks. Students can come in and volunteer 15–20 minutes at a time during one recess a week. This has little impact on the classroom and only requires them to give up one recess a week but still provides a chance for students to help. If each recess time has 5 to 6 students working, that means over 30 students each week who could volunteer in the library media center. Training time will be critical at the beginning of the year, but students can quickly become self-sufficient.

Partnerships

While the library media center could be isolating, there is opportunity to branch out. Technology brings us the ability to connect with others without even leaving the school building. Library media specialists can use their network of library media specialists to bring new projects and opportunities to students. Distance learning is nothing new in today's schools; however, the advances of technology have made it so much easier to connect. There are many free resources that our students and teachers can take advantage to use. One element in both the American Association of School Librarians (AASL) *Standards for the 21st Century Learner* and the International Society for Technology in Education (ISTE) *National Educational Technology Standards for Students* is that students should expand their networks and work globally. Partnering beyond the library helps to bring the world to the students and the students to the world.

Other Schools

If the library media specialist subscribes to any of the various library listservs (see Appendix B for a list of listservs), he is bound to see postings of library media specialists looking to connect with other schools. Just the other day a library media specialist was looking for a school willing to connect using Skype and have a discussion/debate.

The concept of pen pals has been expanding as the modes for communication have been exploding. Blogs, wikis, and podcasts all provide ways for students to communicate from any place in the world. For example, library media specialists and classroom teachers could create a wiki, and students in multiple classrooms, schools, and states could contribute information to build the site. There are also organizations like the Center for Interactive Learning (http://www.cilc.org) or ePals (http://www.epals.com), where library media specialists can search for video conferencing content and partners.

Public Libraries

Public libraries can also be a source of collaboration. Often their budgets and resources will exceed those available in a school library. Building a good relationship with the local library can provide a foundation for sharing resources—both print and online. The following are just a few ways you can collaborate with your local public library.

Interlibrary Loan (ILL)

The most common use for the public library would be for the school to borrow additional books. These titles could be available to students to use in the school library. In one district, each school library has a library card. The library media specialist can request materials by searching the public library online catalog. Twice a week the interschool mail truck stops at the public library to pick up any resources that are waiting to be used in the schools. Then, when the school is finished with the materials, the truck returns them to the public library.

Databases

Purchasing online databases can get quite expensive. The public library and school library could work together to get a discounted price, or make sure that students could use their library cards at school to access the databases available at the public library. Providing similar resources at both types of libraries can be a smooth transition for students using the public library since the resources will be similar to those available at the school library.

Work with financial personnel at both locations to determine how to get the best pricing. The school and public library might consider forming a consortium to work with vendors. Also investigate library consortium in the state. There may already be cooperatives the school can join to save funds on databases, supplies, and so forth.

Programming

Bringing in a poet, author, or other performer? Perhaps the public library would like to connect and have the storyteller work one evening at the public library. How about a one-book, one-community event? It could be the perfect opportunity for the school and public library to promote everyone reading the same book or author. With events like that, the school and public library could work together. Perhaps the school finds appropriate titles on the same subject for younger readers.

Library Media Advisory Committee

Library media specialists need to interact with library users before making decisions that could affect the entire school. A library advisory board is a group consisting of the library media specialist, building administrator, teachers, and maybe parents or a student, who meet from time to time to develop a long-range plan, discuss policies and procedures, and work to solve any issues related to the library media program.

This group acts as an advisor to the library media specialist and principal. It allows the various groups to have some input in the decisions that are made. The library media committee is not the final decision maker; rather, it provides a forum for various stakeholders to share their feelings, thoughts, and ideas. This builds ownership for people in the library media program because they are helping to shape it. For example, the group might discuss the viability of increasing the number of items children can check out. They might look at the school improvement plan and determine ways the library media program supports the plan.

Setting up an Advisory Committee

It may be difficult to get the entire group together, especially if trying to coordinate with the schedule of parents. Consider meeting right before school so parents could participate before they go to work, or maybe meet right before a PTO meeting when parents are already planning to be in the building. Technology also provides ways to participate, so the group might use Skype or other similar products so parents could call into the meeting, or perhaps the meetings might work well virtually using e-mail, a wiki, blog, Moodle, or other online tool, too. Depending on the topic, a quick e-mail could go out and input could be quickly collected so that a decision could be made.

In most elementary schools, the easiest way to set up the committee is to ask for a representative from each grade level, related arts teachers, and a special education teacher. One school opted to merge their technology committee and make it one group (Media/Technology Advisory Committee). This one committee could then talk about both topics because they are interrelated.

Advisory committees may also include parents and/or students depending on the grade configuration of the school and what kind of issues the committee is discussing. Bringing in the perspective from students and parents is always good because sometimes the outside looking in can see things the inside looking out is missing.

In elementary schools, students may not be quite ready to be an active participant on a committee of adults. However, there are still ways to solicit their ideas and needs. Form a small advisory committee and invite them to eat lunch in the library media center once a month. Each month might have a different focus topic. Share it with the students ahead of time so they can be thinking of ideas. Perhaps one month the focus is on what kind of new books should the library media specialist be searching for to add to the collection. Or, another month, the conversation might center on activities to promote National School Library Media Month in April.

Another group idea that could be worth considering is creating a friends of the library group. Very similar to the role that a PTA/PTO takes on for the entire school, the friends group could be a driving force to raise funds, solicit volunteers, and overall be a strong advocate for the school library media center. Check out the Association for Library Trustees, Advocates, Friends, and Foundations, a division of the American Library Association (http://www.ala.org/ala/mgrps/divs/altaff/index.cfm), for more information on how to start up a friends group.

Finally, with whatever kinds of committees or groups are formed, make sure that the committee has a wide variety of personalities. It would be pointless to have a committee where everyone has the same opinion. Put some of those people on the committee who aren't strong library users. This just may be the opportunity needed to get them on board.

The library media specialist's job requires one to work with people of all types. One of the number of things a library media specialist can do to be successful is to build bridges to all her colleagues. Show them the power and potential of what can happen by working with the library media specialist! Amazing things will happen!

Wiki Wrap-Up

The job of the library media specialist is very unique in a school because there are few positions where someone has to work with every person in the building. Working with such a range of people and personalities can be both exciting and stressful. The important thing is knowing what each group needs and working to see how the library media program can help them fulfill those needs. For additional resources, check out the companion wiki Web site (http://www.carl-harvey.com/librarytieswiki/).

Works Cited

All Things PLC. *All Things PLC: Research, Education Tools and Blog for Building a Professional Learning Community.* May 9, 2009, http://www.allthingsplc.info/about/aboutPLC.php.

American Association of School Librarians. *Standards for the 21st Century Learner.* Chicago: American Association of School Librarians, 2007.

Hartzell, Gary. *Building Influence for the School Librarian: Tenets, Targets, and Tactics* (2nd ed.). Columbus, OH: Linworth Publishing, 2003.

International Society for Technology in Education. *National Educational Technology Standards for Students* (2nd ed.). Eugene, OR: International Society for Technology in Education, 2007.

Lance, Keith Curry, Marcia J. Rodney, and Becky Russell. *How Students, Teachers, and Principals Benefit from Strong School Libraries.* Indianapolis, IN: Association for Indiana Media Educators, 2007.

Loertscher, David V. *The Library Media Specialist's Taxonomy* (2nd ed.). San Jose, CA: Hi Willow Research and Publishing, 2000.

Warlick, David. "The Art and Technique of Personal Learning Networks." *David Warlick's CoLearners Wiki.* August 31, 2008, http://davidwarlick.com/wiki/pmwiki.php/Main/TheArtAmpTechniqueOfCultivatingYourPersonalLearningNetwork.

CHAPTER 3

Communication

One of the most important reasons that we communicate is to affect the behavior of other people.

—David F. Warlick, from *Redefining Literacy 2.0* (2nd ed.)

Communication is at the heart of any successful library media program. The library media specialist has to be able to clearly articulate the vision of the library media program to a variety of stakeholders, which often requires translation from "libraryese" into something the stakeholders can understand. It also might mean making multiple translations because each group has their own priorities, so it is important to show the library media program as it most affects them.

Sometimes it is easy to assume that people see what the library media program is doing for kids and why it is important. The reality is that sometimes they have no idea. Therefore, it is essential to provide them with plenty of information in multiple formats. Talking face-to-face with someone is often an easy way to get one's message to him or her, but looking at communication through the 21st-century window, how can these new tools be used to talk with stakeholders? Gary Hartzell notes that people remember their library media program from when they were in school (Hartzell 94). This can be both good and bad. If that was not a positive experience (or was a long time ago), the library media specialist will have to help paint them an image of what a 21st-century library media program looks like. The library media specialist needs to leave no doubt that library media programs are a vital part of the school learning culture.

The previous chapter was organized around the people with whom the library media program interacts. This chapter is organized by what vehicle the library media specialist might use to deliver messages to the various stakeholders. Choosing the vehicle is based solely on how the audience best receives the information. It may vary from group to group, and likely the library media specialist will need to use a variety of communication strategies to get his or her message out.

Vehicles of Communication
Face-to-Face

One of the best ways to communicate is face-to-face. While e-mails might be faster, they lack the emotion and tone of the person's voice or body language. Also, some topics may be sensitive enough that having the information in print may not be wise.

Each administrator has a different style for how they operate. Some administrators have what is commonly called the open-door policy. If the library media specialist walks past the principal's office door and it is open, she knows she is free to interrupt to ask questions or have a conversation. If the door is closed, then the library media specialist will need to find another time to talk. Typically open-door policies mean there is greater access to the administrator. Oftentimes in one day the administrator may have multiple conversations with the library media specialist on a wealth of topics.

The same can be said for conversations when the administrator comes to the library media center. If the library media specialist is not currently teaching a class, it may prove a good time for a conversation with the administrator. Many administrators make daily walks through the building and go into each space where children are learning. If it is hard to catch them with their open door policy, catching the administrator on the instructional walkthrough might be another opportunity.

Finally, some administrators like schedules, appointments, and routine. They may not like to be interrupted. Depending on the administrator and library media specialist, it may be wise to schedule a weekly or biweekly meeting to align calendars, discuss issues, and look ahead to future events.

Another group with whom face-to-face meetings work well is teachers. While planning for instruction can happen over e-mail, a face-to-face conversation often works better to make sure the lesson has been completely thought out—especially for a project being done the first time. Some grade levels will meet together each week to plan out their next week's lessons. This is a perfect time for the library media specialist to join in. He can offer suggestions and ideas for the teachers to think about as they are planning.

At the beginning of each school year, most buildings host a back-to-school night. The schedule and format vary, but the point is to get parents into the school to give them a preview of the year ahead. At one such school, each grade level does a one-hour presentation. It takes three nights to get them all completed, but the library media specialist attends and talks at each one of those meetings. She explains circulation policies to the parents, talks about some of the collaborative projects that their children will be experiencing in the coming years, shares passwords for accessing library databases from home, and puts out a call for volunteers to help in the library media center. This face-to-face meeting is a positive and perfect opportunity to connect with parents. See Figure 3.1 for a sample of library flyer for parent night.

ELEMENTARY SCHOOL LIBRARY MEDIA CENTER

The mission of the Elementary Library Media Center is to prepare students for life-long learning, informed decision making, a love of reading, and the use of information technologies.

Elementary Library Media Center operates on an open access schedule. Students may come to the library media center at any time—individually, in small groups, or with their entire class—to check out and return materials, to read for pleasure or information, to hear stories, or research topics for reports, using a variety of resources.

Collaborative Instruction

Instruction comes from the library media specialist and the classroom teacher coplanning to create lessons that incorporate the *Standards for the 21st Century Learner* with the academic standards, in order to create authentic learning. By working together, both the library media specialist and the classroom teachers are able to work with students as they use information and technology. Our lessons and projects help prepare students for the 21st century by helping them become effective users of information and technology.

Online Databases

You can access online resources such as our computer catalog, student Web links (great for homework help), and library information at: http://www.elementary.k12.state.us/ Please notice the textbook along the right side for password log in for at-home access to our online resources.

Special Programming

+ The library media program provides an annual visit from a children's author with funding provided by PTO. In addition, the library media center hosts two book fairs and a variety of other special events and programming throughout the year.

+ The State Library Association sponsors the State Book Award Program. Students who read or are read 12 of the 20 picture book titles, and students who read or are read 5 of the 20 intermediate titles by May 1 are eligible to vote for the title they liked best.

+ Join the Elementary Library Media Center Birthday Book Club and celebrate a child's birthday (or the birthday of someone special to him or her). Bring in $5 to the library media center and he or she can choose a book to donate to our school from those selected by the library media specialist. The child's name will be written in the book as a way to thank him or her.

Library Media Center Procedures

Number of Items: Students are limited to the number of items for which they can be responsible!

Check-Out Time Limit: Students may keep items for one week (chapter books for two weeks). Students are encouraged to return the items to the library media center as soon as they are finished so they can check out new ones!

Overdue Fines: There are no fines; however, students must return overdue items before new items may be checked out.

Lost Books: Students who lose or damage items beyond repair will be charged the replacement cost of the book. Parents may give permission for their children to check out more items while lost books are being sought by contacting Mr. Booker. Students who habitually lose books and do not pay for them will be limited to using items only at school.

Making Good Choices: The library media program strives to teach our students to be independent reading consumers. If you notice your child is bringing home materials at an inappropriate high or low level of difficulty, please discuss this with your child.

Volunteers

The library media center is always looking for adult volunteers to help shelve books, prepare new materials, and other tasks. If you are interested in helping, please contact one of our media technology assistants at 111.1111 ext. 111.

Questions or Comments?

Please contact Mr. Booker, library media specialist at 111.1111, ext. 110 or mr.booker@elementary.k12.state.us

---

Database Passwords

World Book Online

Login:

Password:

PebbleGo

Login:

Password:

TeachingBooks.net

Login:

Password:

BookFlix

Login:

Password:

Figure 3.1   Parent night library flyer.

Besides back-to-school night, most schools also have a PTA or PTO that helps support the school. These organizations of dedicated parents and teachers are the groups that organize, run, and fund countless programs in the school. They support the school with volunteers, enrichment programming, and are the go-to people when the school needs additional support or help. These groups are also a potential funding source for the library media center, so at one school the library media specialist attends the meetings each month. From time to time, she shares some of the programs going on in the library and thanks the PTA/PTO for supporting them.

Finally, another opportunity for interacting face-to-face is during professional development. In one school, the library media specialist tries to attend all the trainings put on by the literacy coach. These sessions often become ideal opportunities for collaboration planning and curriculum development. By being there at the trainings, the library media specialist has a voice to share ideas and work with the teachers and literacy coach.

Print

In the 21st century, the advent of technology and the green movement have caused us to rethink the use of paper. The amount of money saved, in addition to the amount of trees saved, have made library media specialists and school administrators rethink things like a traditional newsletter to faculty, a newsletter sent home to students, or a monthly/annual report to administrators. This is not to say that all those items have gone away but rather that the library media specialist has been looking at alternative ways to share that same information. By looking for alternative ways, the library media specialist can showcase technology skills while at the same time model being green and doing his or her part to help save the environment.

Sometimes paper is still the best way to get the message home with students. One library media specialist, when starting a new research project with students, will send home a half sheet of links to the LMC Web site and databases. This reminds parents of all the online resources (including any passwords to access databases at home) and guides both students and parents to the library media center Web page, so that students who work at home will still be guided to the right resources. Students can staple this into their research folder or assignment notebook for easy access.

E-Mails

Educators are blasted today with e-mails of all kind from all types of people—administrators, parents, students, and, yes, even the library media specialist. It has become a vital link to everyone in the school. While some educators are more conscientious about reading their e-mail than others are, the same could be said for the newsletters that used to be copied onto paper. E-mail is not any less effective but is rather just another way to send out the information.

E-mail can be used as a tool to deliver important information like schedules, overdue notices, and so forth. It can also be a tool to provide professional development as well as a way to highlight new resources available in the library media center. See Figure 3.2 for e-mail examples.

Schedules for enrichment programs, notices about technology problems, or just an FYI that overdue notices are going home are some of the countless uses for staff e-mail. It is a quick and easy way to send to everyone the details they need to be aware of for a variety of topics.

To: Principal

From: Library Media Specialist

CC: Classroom Teacher

Re: Awesome Project

Just wanted to share what a great project we did with Mr. Jones's classes this week. His students came up with something about the Civil War they wanted to know more about. Each day their class came to the library to work on their projects. Students really had to think about what terms to use while searching for information on their individual projects. I can't wait to see their final projects when they share them in a couple of weeks. You are welcome to join us in the library to listen to their final presentations.

Thanks,

Library Media Specialist

Tips for E-Mailing Your Administrator

✦ Keep e-mails short and on one topic.

✦ Phrase all requests in a manner of "How will this benefit kids?"

✦ Invite the administrator to the library media center often.

✦ Make sure that all your e-mails are not negative; share good news, too!

✦ Make sure to cc (carbon copy) teachers on e-mails you send the administrator praising them.

✦ Cc the principal on e-mails when you send new resources, new books, tips, and ideas.

✦ For sensitive topics or when the potential to be misunderstood is apparent, send an e-mail requesting to speak in person.

✦ If you are writing an e-mail in response to a problem or concern and you are upset or angry, make sure *not* to send it right away. Take time to cool down and rewrite.

To: All Staff

From: Library Media Specialist

Re: Weekly Web Site

This week's Web site I think I have shared before, but it is worth repeating.

✦ Wish you could track all the books your class reads this school year?

✦ Wish you could remember that great book about responsibility that you read last year?

✦ Wish you could post comments, notes, or ideas about books to refresh your memory?

Use http://www.librarything.com

See my example below, where I have marked the book I read to a class of Kindergarteners today. I added a tag of Kindergarten08 to remind me when I read it last. I can keep adding all year. Just think how powerful it would be for kids to see that list grow and grow as you read books. Use your TV to project your computer as you add titles, and older students could add books as they are at stations or under supervision of the teacher. There are lots of great possibilities.

Happy Surfing!

Academic Standards: English/Language Arts

School Improvement Plan: Literacy

Ideas for E-Mails to Send to Teachers:

✦ Weekly Web site

✦ Highlight a new book and ways to use it

✦ Directed e-mails to grade levels or departments with new resources

✦ Directed e-mails to grade levels or departments with ideas for collaborative projects

✦ Monthly newsletter

Figure 3.2 Sample e-mail communication.

Many automation systems now have it as an option to e-mail out overdue notices. Sending them directly to the patron's e-mail box allows them to see what they still have checked out and avoids printing it out on paper. It will be important to research the privacy issues involved with this option, too. Many schools now collect parent e-mail addresses, and that information can easily be imported into the automation system. However, does emailing overdue notices for elementary students violate their privacy rights? Check with the department of education or state library in your state in regards to the rules about public and school records. Do parents (or teachers) have a right to know what their child has checked out from the library media center? It is a fine line in elementary schools between protecting the child's privacy and gaining parental support to locate overdue books or pay for lost items (Adams 35).

Professional development is another option for e-mail. Those monthly newsletters the library media specialist used to run off on the copier are now sent via e-mail instead of printed out. Sent as a PDF file or pasted right into the e-mail itself, the newsletters contain important updates for the faculty, directions for using new pieces of technology, links to Web sites and books that support school improvement goals, and so forth. Newsletters might also contain things like a calendar of author birthdays, important information about new technology, a list of collaborative projects, and so forth. They still need to be short and succinct for staff to read them, but e-mail allows them to be sent without the wasted paper. See Figure 3.3 for a newsletter example.

Other things that can be sent via e-mail include a link to a weekly Web site. Connect it back to the school improvement plan and academic standards. The visual reminder of a great Web site along with how it relates to what is important to the building will show teachers and administrators that the library media program is very aware of the important things happening in the school. One school has a model where teachers ask seven literacy-related questions after reading a text. The library media specialist periodically picks a new book, creates the seven questions, and sends it out to the staff (check out the Web site of these books at http://www.nobl.k12.in.us/media/NorthMedia/teachers/LL/LLReadAlouds.HTM). This gives them a new book they can try and incorporate rather than using the same old, often-heard stories.

Reports to administrators are now on e-mail as well. A monthly report to an administrator might include the following: a list of classes that have collaborated with the library media specialist, a list of administrative tasks completed by the library media specialist and support staff, a calendar of events that happened during the previous month, and a list of upcoming events. Circulation stats are also a good addition to this short report. The annual report also could be sent via e-mail or uploaded onto the Web for all to see. See Figure 3.4 for an example of a monthly report and Figure 3.5 for an example of a year end report.

People are bombarded with e-mails every day, so keep the message short so they quickly can get the information they need.

Library Media Center Web Page

The library media center Web page is an amazing communication opportunity. Initially a one-way format where the library media specialist could share with students, parents, teachers, and administrators, it now can be a dynamic site with two-way communication. A great way to

Month Year ~ Volume 1, Issue 1

Media Matters

(Below are some possible article ideas. You could also use these as headings for blog postings as well. Try to keep your newsletter to one page (front and back). Rotate columns depending on what is happening in your library!)

Collaboration Corner—Share the great projects happening in your library media center—a great place to recognize teachers who are working with you.

Coming Soon—Here you can promote upcoming events such as the book fair or author visit.

I Found It on the Web—Share a Web site such as a Web 2.0 tool and how you might use it with students.

A Picture Is Worth a Thousand Words—Highlight a new picture book and how you might use it in the classroom.

It's a Novel Idea—Highlight a new novel and how you might use it in the classroom.

Media Moments Calendar—Share library events, upcoming projects, and/or author birthdays.

Quotable Quote—Find great quotes from children's literature or quote books to share.

What's New in the Library Media Center?—Print a list of new resources in the library media center. Time this with a new book day where teachers can come down and see the books on the list.

Just the Facts—Share with readers some stats about the library. How many books have been checked out? How many classes have used the library?

Clip It; Save It!—Share a short professional development tip such as how to use a database or the library computer catalog.

Examples:

Deer Lakes Middles School, Russellton, Pennsylvania

http://www.deerlakes.net/modules.php?name=ms&file=lnews

New Providence Elementary School, Lexington, South Carolina

http://www.npeslibrary.com/newsletters.html

Gaskill Preparatory School, Niagara Falls, New York

http://www.nylearns.org/webpage/viewpage.aspx?ID=116070&UID=27533

Figure 3.3 Newsletters.

Library Media Center ~ Principal Update	
Date: _____	

Collaboration
  ✦ Kindergarten—
  ✦ 1st Grade—
  ✦ 2nd Grade—
  ✦ 3rd Grade—
  ✦ 4th Grade—
  ✦ Related Arts, Special Education—
	In this box include all the collaborative lessons and projects. This is a great place to mention teachers who are working with the library media specialist.

General Media/Tech Information
  ✦
  ✦
  ✦
  ✦
	In this box include administrative tasks and work and projects. Make sure to include the work your support staff is doing as well.

Professional Activities
  ✦
  ✦
  ✦
  ✦
  ✦
	In this box highlight conferences and workshops attended, visitors to your library media center, articles published, etc.

Upcoming Activities
  ✦
  ✦
  ✦
  ✦
  ✦
	In this box, give a preview of the month ahead. This could include projects, special events, or workshops you are attending or presenting.

Library Media Center Statistics	Broken Down by Month—Student Circulation		In this box, include some statistics. These will vary depending on the level and your administrator. Use those statistics that speak to your school improvement goals.
Faculty: _____ (___ / 50 staff member) Students:_____ (___ / 460 student) Classes in for Instruction: _____	August		
	September		
	October		
	November		
	December		
	January		
	February		
	March		
	April		
	May		

Other Samples of Monthly Reports

Creekview High School, Canton, Georgia

    http://webtech.cherokee.k12.ga.us/creekview-hs/MediaCenter/monthly_reports.htm

Chicago Public Schools, Chicago, Illinois

    http://www.cps.k12.il.aboutcps/departments/libraries/pdf/LibraryMediaCenterMonthlyReport.doc

Figure 3.4 Principal monthly report.

Briefly summarize one collaborative project you started this school year.

What connections has the library media program made to building the school improvement plan?

+ Literacy

+ Math

What role has the library media program played in professional development?

What were some of the major highlights from this school year?

What plans/goals are planned for the library media program?

Our goals for next year include:

Just the Facts

How many total items circulated this year?	
To students?	
To staff?	
Leveled libraries?	
How many classes used the library media center facility? (Total number)	
How many collaborative projects, units, or lessons between the library media specialist and classroom teacher?	

Other Examples:

Suggestions and Ideas from Teacher Librarian Ning

http://teacherlibrarian.ning.com/forum/topic/show?id=672799%3ATopic%3A4267&x=1&page=1

Legacy High School, Broomfield, Colorado

http://legacy.adams12.org/webpages/library/Documents/2008AnnualReport.pdf

Springfield Township High School, Springfield, Pennsylvania

http://www.sdst.org/shs/library/documents/annualreport08.pdf

Figure 3.5   Year end report.

examine a variety of school library Web sites is to check out the webquest (http://schoollibrary websites.wikispaces.com) by Joyce Valenza. See other examples in Figure 3.6

The classic school library Web site has a link to the school library catalog, links for student projects, links to databases, and a space to advertise library events. The 21st-century library media center Web page would also include a blog to post activities, resources, and other library-related news. It would use wikis to organize links for students, so that both teachers and students could add to the list as they locate additional resources. Podcasts could also be posted of students sharing what they've found in their research.

Larry Johnson and Annette Lamb on their Web site (http://eduscapes.com/arch/ia/research2i. htm) have posted as part of a course they teach—Information Architecture for the Web—a list of ideas of potential items to include on a school or library Web site. They also have a list of school library Web sites (http://eduscapes.com/arch/evaluate/archschool.html) that would be good places for library media specialists to explore as they design their own Web site.

Peter Milbury created one of the earliest directories of school library media centers on the Web. (a few years ago he passed the baton to keep the site current to others, so it remains active and updated at http://www.school-libraries.net). This directory has links to school library Web sites all over the United States and the world and is certainly worth a look when determining what resources the library media center Web site should have.

Blogs and wikis might also be a format to consider to use when setting up a library media center Web site. The ease of use and ability to quickly update them could make the format a great choice as the set-up for a library media center Web page. Check district policies about setting up Web sites, blogs, wikis, and so forth on space other than that owned by the district. Some schools have procedures and policies in place that will need to be followed or reviewed before starting a project.

Web 2.0

One media specialist makes a packet every year for the teachers, giving them all the information they need about library media procedures. Next year, the packet is going from a print version to a wiki where teachers will be able to quickly access the information all year long. See Figure 3.7 for a listing of what was in the back-to-school packet.

A blog is another way to communicate with stakeholders. Post events, book reviews, outstanding projects, and so forth. The blog is another tool that could augment the library media center newsletter and widen the audience beyond just the faculty (see Appendix C for examples).

Have students record a weekly podcast of happenings in the library media center. Students could have their own talk radio show and highlight some of the resources, projects, and events happening in the library media center (see Appendix C for examples).

These online tools provide a plethora of new options for sharing what is happening in the library media center. Take advantage of them not only as a tool for students to express their learning but also as a vehicle to get out the positive message about the library media center.

Elements to consider including:

+ Student resources

+ Teacher resources

+ Parent resources

+ Online catalog

+ Online databases

+ Online tools

+ Library media resources

+ Links to Web 2.0 tools like
  podcasts, blogs, and wikis

+ Current Events

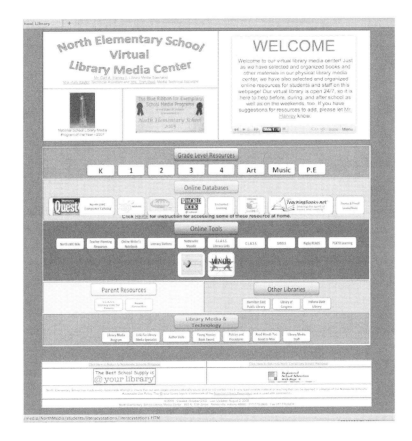

Examples:

    Grandview Elementary, Spring Valley, New York

        http://www.grandviewlibrary.org/

    Naples High School, Naples, Florida

        http://www.collierschools.com/nhs/lmc/

    North Elementary Library Media Center, Noblesville, Indiana

        http://www.nobl.k12.in.us/media/northmedia/index.htm

    Springfield Township High School, Erdenheim, Pennsylvania

        http://www.sdst.org/shs/library/

Directories of School Library Web Sites:

    School Libraries.Net

        http://www.school-libraries.net

Joyce Valenza's WebQuest about School Library Web Sites:

    http://schoollibrarywebsites.wikispaces.com/

Figure 3.6   Library media center Web page.

Library Media Center ~ Back-to-School Packet

Here are some examples of resources to give teachers and staff at the beginning of the year. This gives them a quick reference guide to library media and technology resources.

Quick Reference Guide for Teachers and Staff

Table of Contents

Information

- ✦ Library Media Program Procedures and Fact Sheet
- ✦ Important Dates
- ✦ Library Media and Technology—Who Do I Ask?
- ✦ What Can a Teacher Expect of a Library Media Specialist?
- ✦ North Library Media Center Reading Support Statement
- ✦ What Does Big6 Research Look Like in an Elementary School?

Instructional Resources

- ✦ Media/Technology Integration Guide or Curriculum
- ✦ Textbook Procedures
- ✦ Leveled Library Procedures
- ✦ Technology Resources (Software and Hardware)
- ✦ Guide to Online Resources
  - ✦ Library Media Center Web Page
  - ✦ Library Computer Catalog
  - ✦ State-Wide Databases
  - ✦ World Book Online
  - ✦ TeachingBooks.net
  - ✦ Enchanted Learning
  - ✦ United Streaming
  - ✦ Visual Thesaurus
  - ✦ Atomic Learning
  - ✦ Reading A to Z Leveled Books
  - ✦ Fountas and Pinnell Leveled Books
  - ✦ Schools Blogs
  - ✦ State Book Award Nominees
- ✦ Quick Online Reference Guide to Stick to Computer

Figure 3.7 Teacher back-to-school packet.

Video

Library media centers that have a morning announcement show can use that to advertise what is happening in the library media center. Promote an author coming to visit or book talk some of the new titles in this year's book fair. Videos can be filmed and posted on the Web for others to learn what is happening at school, too.

Make sure that any video posted to the Web adheres to copyright guidelines. Putting information out on the Web is a public performance, so any music should be royalty free, and the students must have created any images or text. If there are any items that are copyrighted, they need to be edited out or permission from the copyright holder needs to be granted before posting them online.

Wiki Wrap-Up

Library media specialists need to take advantage of all the communication tools in their arsenals. These tools are the vehicle to get the message out about what the library media program does and how it affects student achievement. Communication is critical for working with a variety of stakeholders. As for the 21st century brings new tools and communication formats, library media specialists need to look for how these tools can be use to communicate! For additional resources, check out the companion wiki Web site (http://www.carl-harvey.com/librarytieswiki/).

Works Cited

Adams, Helen. "Disclosing Student Records." *School Library Media Activities Monthly.* October 2006, 35.

Hartzell, Gary. *Building Influence for the School Librarian: Tenets, Targets, and Tactics* (2nd ed.). Columbus, OH: Linworth Publishing, 2003.

CHAPTER 4

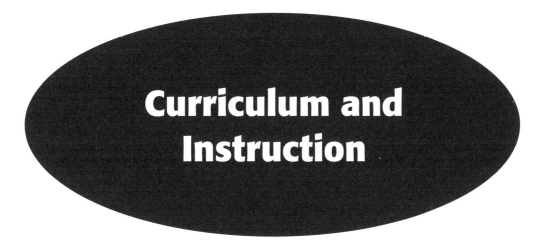

Curriculum and Instruction

We must take every step necessary to put our library media center at the center of the school universe—and the most essential step of all is collaboration.

—Toni Buzzeo, "Collaborating from the Center of the School Universe"

The instructional component of the library media program continues to grow and expand. The new American Association of School Librarians' (AASL) *Empowering Learners: Guidelines for School Library Media Programs* outlines the mission of the library media program to help students (and staff) be prepared for finding, using, evaluating, creating, and sharing information.

Collaborative Teaching

A few years ago an experienced teacher moved to a new school district. Each Monday, his grade level would sit down to plan out the next week. In addition to the 4th-grade teachers, the library media specialist and special education teacher also attended the planning sessions. While he was used to collaborating with the other teachers at his grade level, he was amazed to see the connection between the library media specialist and special education teachers. Not only were they there just to listen about the week ahead, but they also contributed ideas and strategies. They scheduled research projects, considered ideas for ways to use technology, maximized their use of resources, and worked together as a team for the students. Finally after about a month, he looked at the others who had been joining the planning and said, "Do you guys come every week?" In his prior school there had been no interaction with the library media specialist or resource teachers. This was a new environment for him. He so appreciated the team approach to their lesson planning and the influence the resource teachers and the library media specialist have on their planning, so it was a pleasant surprise for him.

Collaboration has been a recognized part of library media programs since *Information Power* made its debut in 1988. Collaboration, as defined by Toni Buzzeo in *The Collaboration Handbook,* is when "the partners have a prolonged and interdependent relationship. They share goals, have carefully defined roles in the process, and plan much more comprehensively. Units and projects are team-planned, team-taught, and team-assessed" (Buzzeo 30). There is so much power in what can be offered to students by combining the skills, knowledge, and expertise of the library media specialist and the classroom teacher. Collaboration is a two-way street. While just starting out, it often seems like the library media specialist is the one driving and pushing to work with teachers, but once the model is in place and there is an understanding of the potential, teachers come to the library media specialist to plan projects.

One of the obstacles to collaboration often mentioned is the library media center schedule. The debate about flexible versus fixed scheduling has long been raging in the field. Chapter 7 of this book talks more about the battle of reality versus ideal, but no matter what type of schedule exists in the library media center, collaboration is critical for student learning. The model of teaching library skills in isolation is not effective.

No matter what schedule the library media program operates on, teachers and library media specialists should be working together. The same applies to related arts teachers (art, music, and physical education). It can be very powerful for students when everyone plans together. Powerful connections can be made. For example, consider the following scenario. All of these teachers sat down together to plan a unit focused around the pond biome. The overarching science standards were the link. Each teacher was able to take his or her own standards to adapt and design content around a centralized theme. These connections provided a learning experience for students where everything related to each other. The following is a quick summary of what it looked like in the various rooms.

+ **In the classroom:** Students complete a K-W-L (What do I know?, What do I want to know?, What did I learn?) chart about frogs and pond life. They take this with them to their other related arts classes to see if they can make connections to art, music, physical education, and so forth.

+ **In art:** Students talk about color and perspective by creating images of frogs.

+ **In music:** Students use instruments to recreate sounds heard around a pond. They access a database such as PebbleGo to find what their animals sound like.

+ **In physical education:** Students try to mimic how animals around the pond move (jumping, hoping, crawling, flying, etc.). Students work in teams to create an exercise to teach the whole school based on a pond animal.

+ **In the library media center:** Students research about frogs and determine what they have to have in their environment to survive. Students then choose another animal to research and have to determine whether their animal would survive in the pond environment or not. They share their findings on the class wiki.

+ **In the computer lab:** Students develop a blog where they can post what they've learned and begin to think about ways to protect the frog's habitat or environment.

Original Post	10	5	0
	The student posted a complete response. It included details from his/her research. His/her opinions were supported with data.	The student posted a reasonable response. It included some details from his/her research. His/her opinions, however, were not supported with data.	The student did not post a complete response. There were no facts from his/her research.
Comments	10	5	0
	The student used data to respond to his/her classmates' posts. He/she responded to at least 10 of his/her classmates.	The student used data to respond to his/her classmates' posts. He/she responded to at least 5 of his/her classmates.	The student did not use data to respond to his/her classmates' posts. He/she responded to less than 5 people.
Responsibility	10	5	0
	All of the student's replies were appropriate. He/she was respectful when dissenting and treated his/her classmates with respect.	Most of the student's replies were appropriate. He/she was respectful when dissenting and treated his/her classmates with respect.	The student did not reply appropriately. He/she was disrespectful to his/her classmates.
Student's Total Score			

Figure 4.1 Sample assessment rubric.

+ **Back in the classroom:** Students talk about fact/fiction, reading text of both kinds based on frogs. Students also reflect on what they've learned and determine if there is still more information they need.

+ **Assessment:** The classroom teacher, library media specialist, and related arts teachers all assesses students' progress during this unit. Each project has a rubric developed by the teacher, but it is shared with other teachers on the team. So, for example, in the computer lab their was a rubric like the one in Figure 4.1. Where there is overlap, both teachers assess the projects together. At the end of the project, the teachers reflect on what changes they may want or need to make to the unit next year.

With all these examples, the learning is connected for the kids. There was a reason for what they were learning. It gave them a deep connection and better understanding. Units like this one require someone to start the idea and take the lead. The library media specialist is the perfect connector for bringing everyone together.

Getting Started with Collaboration

To collaborate you have to build trust between the collaborators. Classroom teachers have to feel that they can trust the library media specialist to deliver on what they promise. Collaboration tends to begin with small one-time lessons. Rarely does one jump right in with a multiday, multilayered project. It takes time to build those relationships to where teachers feel comfortable working with the media specialist on the bigger projects.

The beginning of collaboration often feels like a one-way street. The library media specialist must take initiative to be out there promoting ideas and projects. The library media specialist has to be asking questions.

+ What topics are coming up in your plans?

+ What areas could we use more resources on in the library media center?

+ How can I support what you are teaching in the classroom?

+ How can we work together to design a project?

+ I had an idea, what do you think of this?

+ How can I help you integrate technology?

These questions might be asked while passing a teacher in the hallway, while eating lunch in the cafeteria, while a teacher has her class checking out books in the library media center, while teachers are sitting down and planning, while teachers are meeting to develop long-range plans/curriculum, or sent over the school e-mail system.

Attitude is important during these discussions. There will be teachers who don't like the ideas presented, don't want to work with the library media specialist, or just have a very cavalier attitude about the whole thing. While that may be the attitude of the teacher, for the sake of the students, the library media specialist must persevere. Continue to offer ideas and suggestions. Continue to communicate with teachers (even those who don't seem as interested). Continue to make it known that the library media specialist is there and wants to be a partner. It may take some time, but even the most reluctant teachers will eventually come around. The pressure from seeing what their peers are doing is a great way to open up reluctant teachers to collaboration.

Administrators who see the benefits of collaboration may also help encourage reluctant teachers to work with the library media center. A little encouragement from an administrator can go a long way to get even the most reluctant teacher down to the library media center.

When starting a new job (or even a new school year) ask to sit down with each grade level either during their prep or after school. Get administrator support for these meetings. Be prepared ahead of time with an agenda (see Figure 4.2 for an example of a possible agenda) with one or two major topics for discussion.

Use this time to make introductions, share the concept of collaborative planning, and provide some examples. Allow teachers to give feedback (be prepared that not everything they say will be music to the library media specialist's ears). Try to develop a way to work with their concerns or suggestions. Ask them about one thing they liked best about the library media program and one thing they wish they could change. Type up notes and share them with the grade level and administrators. These introductions can be a successful beginning to open a dialogue. The library media program is not all about the library media specialist. Input from others only helps to make the program stronger.

In the years that follow, there may not be a need to do the formal meetings. However, the library media specialist may want to make sure to do this with new teachers every year. It is easier to present some of this information in small groups rather than in a staff meeting. In staff meetings it can feel like it is the library media specialist versus the world. Small groups make it a more manageable and personal discussion. Professional learning communities (PLCs) are another great way to meet with teachers in small groups.

Next, determine how the teachers plan their lessons each week. Here are some possible scenarios:

✦ Teachers plan alone.

✦ Teachers plan alone but have a grade-level curriculum map to guide them.

✦ Teachers plan together as a grade level and have a grade-level curriculum map to guide them.

✦ Teachers plan as a grade-level team along with other teachers (special education, library media, etc.).

If the grade level has them, the library media specialist needs a copy of the curriculum map or yearlong plan. These documents tend to sometimes be in a constant state of flux, so at the beginning of each year, ask for the most current edition. Keep them in a binder (or saved to the computer) for easy reference. Some districts also post their curriculum on the district Web page or adopt the statewide curriculum. Whether the curricula are online or in print, the library media specialist needs to get them. These can not only help guide development of collaborative projects but also give valuable information to assist with collection development. These guides may only be the standards to be covered, but teachers may take those and develop themes and units in a yearlong plan.

Goals:

⇒ To begin to work together.

⇒ To begin a long-range plan for collaboration.

Flexible Agenda:

Introductions

✦ Name, grade level.

✦ What is your favorite children's author/book?

Something Old, Something New

✦ What do you like best about the library media center?

✦ If you could change one thing about the library media center, what would it be?

Long-Term Planning

✦ Calendar—rough timeline for what themes/units you use to teach.

✦ Collection development—Where do we need more resources?

Resources:

✦ Academic Standards

✦ *Standards for 21st Century Learner*

✦ *National Education Technology Standards for Students*

✦ Media/Technology Benchmarks

✦ Software/Technology Available

Figure 4.2 Sample introduction meeting agenda.

If teachers plan alone, using those yearlong planning guides will be important. The library media specialist will need to utilize e-mail and face-to-face conversations to begin collaborating with teachers. If teachers plan together as a grade level, ask them when they meet and then ask to join them. Some teams will plan during their prep, some will plan before school, and some will plan after school. See Figure 4.3 for a sample of a weekly planning schedule. Keep in mind there is one library media specialist and anywhere from five to seven or more grade levels depending on the configuration of the school. When beginning to collaborate, pick one or two grade levels to focus on making connections. Attend those planning sessions as frequently as possible. It may be impossible to attend every planning session, every week. But certainly the library media specialist should strive for that goal. The more information the library media specialist has, the easier it is to make connections. When the library media specialist is unable to attend the planning meetings, let the teachers know and ask beforehand if there is anything you can do to help.

As time progresses, the library media specialist can move to focus on other grade levels and spend more time at their planning sessions. This does not mean the library media specialist stops going to the meetings of the other grade levels or that the library media specialist drops the project and lessons he has planned in the past. However, once the library media specialist has built a good relationship with one grade level, he can now spend a little less time with that grade level and a little more time with a grade level that he has not worked with before.

It is important to be a part of those planning discussions as much as possible, but reality dictates that it will be almost impossible to get to every grade level every week. When grade levels plan during their preparation time, it can be really difficult. If the library media specialist cannot attend their planning sessions, ask teachers to copy their plans or send a quick summary of where they are and where they are going (either paper or electronic). A short e-mail or a quick conversation before or after school also can be a good way to find out what teachers are doing in their classrooms. Make sure to stress that the library media specialist needs to know what is happening so she can make connections in the library media center and offer ideas, resources, and project possibilities.

Sustaining Collaboration

Once the door to collaboration is open, the real fun begins. One of the most frequent comments about why people enjoy working in the library media center is because no two days are ever the same. Even projects that were developed several years ago are tweaked and altered each year to improve them and make them better.

The collaboration log helps to sustain collaboration because the library media specialist has documentation from the previous year. He can review the log and keep up with teachers: "Hey, I noticed last year around this time we started project X. Would you like to schedule that again?" Documenting in a collaboration log helps the library media specialist and teacher. It tracks and organizes the entire project.

Continuing to attend the grade-level planning meetings is also important. This constant contact keeps things from being lost in the shuffle. Teachers get busy and sometimes will forget or alter what they are doing each year. Changes in standards, new teachers, and a host of variables can

	Monday	Tuesday	Wednesday	Thursday	Friday
Before school	4th grade	3rd grade			
During prep				2nd grade	
After school		1st grade	Kindergarten		

It is helpful when each grade level plans at a different time. Unfortunately, that is not always feasible or something the library media specialist can control. In cases like that, alternate from week to week or split your time in half for each grade level.

Figure 4.3 Sample planning schedule.

cause changes from year to year. Being present at those meetings provides a reminder of the possibilities and the opportunities available in the library media center.

Praise teachers who have done successful projects with the library media specialist. Send an e-mail to the principal talking about the great project and carbon copy the teacher so he or she can see that the library media specialist is bragging about him or her. In the library media newsletter highlight those teachers who were working with students in the library media center this month. This not only gives a pat on the back to the teachers who were collaborating, but it may just get some of those who are a little resistant to jump on the bandwagon.

Both beginning and maintaining collaboration requires administrative support. Make sure to keep the administrator in the loop about implementing a collaboration model. Show him samples of the lessons and projects so he can see the results of the effort. Once administrators are on board, they can help push the school even more down the collaborative road. They can ask teachers what they have been doing in the library media center. They can encourage the collaborative connections. Their influence can go a long way to help build the collaborative environment.

One day a principal was giving a tour of the school to a principal from another district. The principal shared about the collaborative environment at the school and how the library media program was an active part of it. He talked about how everything was planned as a team. The other principal asked, "How does the library media specialist get the teachers to work with her?" The principal responded, "Well, she doesn't really give us a choice." At first thought, one might think that isn't really collaboration, but in reality that library media specialist had been persistent to the point where she had wiggled her way into the grade levels and now it was just part of how the school operates. It wasn't a choice, but rather was just a part of the learning culture in that school.

The proactive library media specialist will move faster down the road to collaboration. The library media specialist has to (at first) be the one who starts the collaboration discussions. It is unrealistic to think teachers will be breaking down the door to collaborate (unless they have had previous experiences working with a good library media specialist). The library media specialist has to be the one to make that first step. However, once the door is open, then other possibilities develop.

Documenting Collaboration

Keeping track of collaboration experiences is important for a few of reasons. The first is to keep track of what role each participant in the project is playing. What is the teacher teaching? What is the library media specialist teaching? Especially for first-time projects, making sure that everyone is on the same page is important. The second reason is that documentation provides proof of what the library media program offers at the school. The library media specialist can track the number of classes, the number of projects, the numbers of students at each grade level. This can be important data to have available when discussing staffing, budgets, schedules, and so forth. The third reason is to provide a way to reflect on the project for future years. Having documentation can help when one goes to the next year to make the project even better (Loertscher 81–84).

LIBRARY MEDIA CENTER
COLLABORATION PLANNING AND TEACHING LOG

Teacher(s): _____

Grade Level: _____ Planning Date: _____ Project Date:_____

Standards for 21st Century Learner	**Project Description**
1. Inquire, think critically, and gain knowledge. a. Skills: _____ b. Dispositions: _____ c. Responsibilities: _____ d. Self-Assessment: _____ **2. Draw conclusions, make informed decisions, apply knowledge to new situations, and create new knowledge.** a. Skills: _____ b. Dispositions: _____ c. Responsibilities: _____ d. Self-Assessment: _____ **3. Share knowledge and participate ethically and productively as members of our democratic society.** a. Skills: _____ b. Dispositions: _____ c. Responsibilities: _____ d. Self-Assessment: _____ **4. Pursue personal and aesthetic growth.** a. Skills: _____ b. Dispositions: _____ c. Responsibilities: _____ d. Self-Assessment: _____	
Academic Standards	**Teacher Will:**
School Improvement Goals Supported / Strategies Implemented	
Resources ___ Online Resources ___ PowerPoint ___ Word ___ Excel ___ Blog/Wiki ___ Video Production ___ Multimedia Software ___ Inspiration/ Kidspiration ___ Digital Cameras ___ Digital Video Cameras ___ Streaming Video ___ Scanner ___ Other: ___ Other: ___ Other:	**Library Media Specialist Will:**
Evaluation	

Attach any other handouts, notes, or materials created for the project.

Figure 4.4 Collaboration log form.

Figure 4.4 is a sample collaboration form. This collaboration log is based on the new AASL's *Standards for the 21st Century Learner.* The traditional method would be to keep a binder where one would organize the forms based on the school calendar. Behind each form, one would include all the forms, handouts, notes, resources, and so forth for easy access. However, besides paper/ pencil forms, consider electronic methods for collecting and organizing collaboration logs.

✦ Use FileMakerPro or another database program to create fields where data from the collaboration log can be entered.

✦ Use Excel to create a simple spreadsheet of data about each collaborative experience.

✦ Use Word to document each project. Create a document for each grade level or teacher and then just add to the list throughout the year.

✦ Use pbworks (http://www.pbwork.com) or wikispaces (http://www.wikispaces.com) to set up a place where the library media specialist and the teachers can track collaboration. Make sure teachers have access to add to/edit the wiki, too.

✦ Use a folder on the computer to keep all the related files. Organize all the projects into folders for each grade level.

These documents and records can be invaluable. Sometimes a teacher will come and say, "Remember that project we did three years ago?" With the collaboration log, one has the data and information to say, "Why, yes, I do. Here is what was successful and here is where we can make some improvements. Want to try it again?"

Curriculum Development

As states update their content standards, as textbooks change, as new teachers are hired into a grade level, and as new resources become available, there are constant changes and alterations to the curriculum at a grade level. These may be subtle changes that are just altered as a grade level plans each week, or they may require complete overhauls of the yearlong plan. The library media specialist should be a very active part of that planning because there is great potential to influence the plan and to help teach the plan.

Some schools provide their teachers with a day or two each year to work on updating their curriculum, or they give time during the summer. Sometimes this happens without any time or financial support from the district. Teachers will just take it on themselves to work on it during their free time. However the revisions are taking place, the library media specialist should lobby to be included in those planning sessions. During those revisions, there is potential that the library media specialist can provide additional or new resources teachers can use, they can suggest projects that bring in the new AASL's *Standards for 21st Century Learner* and International Society for Technology in Education's (ISTE) *National Educational Standards for Teachers,* and they can help provide ways teachers can utilize technology as part of their plans as well.

These planning sessions work as a two-way communication street because as the curriculum is developed and revised, there is great opportunity to talk about what resources might be needed to meet the needs that arise because of the adjustments. The more advance time the library media specialist has to find the most the resources and the funds with which to purchase them, the more likely it is that the resources can be available when the teachers are ready to implement the revised curriculum.

Consider the school where the principal moved several teachers to different grade levels. One level in particular had all new teachers. The library media specialist made it a priority to attend those planning sessions. The library media specialist was on the ground floor of designing that curriculum, which resulted in successful collaboration experiences.

At another school, the library media specialist sat in on a training session with the literacy coach. The grade level was working through completely revamping their unit from the beginning of the year. This was a great opportunity for the library media specialist to be in on the ground floor of curriculum development. Not only was the unit tied better to the grade level standards, but they were able to create projects that connected to the library media program as well.

Standards

Check out your state's department of education Web site to see the academic standards or benchmarks they have created. The standards vary from state to state. Some states have developed library-specific standards while others have relied on correlating the state standards to the AASL's or ISTE's standards.

The standards and standardized testing are driving the curriculum and what is taught in today's schools. Library media specialists need to know the academic standards and be ready to use them when planning and collaborating with teachers.

National standards also are available for most core subjects as well as from AASL and ISTE. Also check out the Partnership for the 21st Century Skills (P21). These national models for students guide what should be happening in the library media center.

The standards become a framework for teachers designing curriculum. The library media specialist should be the expert on the AASL and ISTE standards, and the teachers should be the experts on the grade-level standards. The experts then can create meaningful opportunities by interweaving the two sets of standards together. At the same time, the library media specialist will become well versed in the state standards, too. It can be very helpful when planning with a grade level if the library media specialist can say, "Well, that's a standard for the next grade level or they should have already mastered that in the previous level." By working with each grade level, the library media specialist gets to see the whole picture of the school.

Sometimes when working with teachers, having a framework is helpful. Sample lessons and ideas of what the standards mean can help create ideas and spark conversation. In Indiana, for example, the department of education has created a Web site with resources that support each academic standard including lesson plans (http://dc.doe.in.gov/Standards/AcademicStandards/resources.aspx). The Illinois Standards Aligned Instruction for Libraries (ISAILS; http://isail.wikidot.com/), which was created by the Illinois School Library Media Association Standards Committee to demonstrate the cross-curricular value of school libraries.

The AASL published *Standards for the 21st Century Learner in Action* to provide examples of what the standards look like at each level. It is unlikely that teachers and library media specialist would implement these projects exactly as written. Rather, they give perspective and provide ideas for creating lessons and units. See Figure 4.5 and Figure 4.6 for examples of collaborative lessons for both primary and intermediate students.

LIBRARY MEDIA CENTER
COLLABORATION PLANNING AND TEACHING LOG

Teacher(s): _____

Grade Level: _____ Primary Grades_____ Planning Date: _____ Project Date:_____

Standards for 21st Century Learner	**Project Description**

Standards for 21st Century Learner

1. **Inquire, think critically, and gain knowledge.**
   a. Skills: _____1.1.1, 1.1.3, 1.1.4, 1.1.6_____
   b. Dispositions: _____1.2.1, 1.2.6_____
   c. Responsibilities: _____1.3.1, 1.3.5_____
   d. Self-Assessment: ___1.4.1, 1.4.4_____

2. **Draw conclusions, make informed decisions, apply knowledge to new situations, and create new knowledge.**
   a. Skills: _____2.1.1, 2.1.3_____
   b. Dispositions: _____
   c. Responsibilities: _____
   d. Self-Assessment: _____

3. **Share knowledge and participate ethically and productively as members of our democratic society.**
   a. Skills: _____3.1.3_____
   b. Dispositions: _____
   c. Responsibilities: _____
   d. Self-Assessment: _____

4. **Pursue personal and aesthetic growth.**
   a. Skills: _____
   b. Dispositions: _____
   c. Responsibilities: _____
   d. Self-Assessment: _____

Project Description

✦ Students will choose an animal from the pond biome. Students will follow the Big6 using a research journal to track and organize their research.

✦ Students will brainstorm a list of questions about their animal.

✦ Students will then have to determine if that animal could live in the rainforest, too. They have to prove their answer based on the facts they found. The evidence must support the answer that they choose.

✦ Students will create a short video commercial about their animal and share why or why it couldn't live in the rainforest.

Timeline:

✦ Two to three visits to the library media center for research.

✦ A couple of days to a week in the classroom to use their research to determine if their animal could live in the rainforest and then write the report with evidence along with the script for the commercial.

✦ They will also need some time in the video studio to put their commercial together.

Academic Standards

English / language arts
Writing

Teacher Will:

✦ Introduce the biomes in the classroom prior to starting the project.

✦ Assist students while they are using the library resources.

✦ Assess the final product.

School Improvement
Goals Supported / Strategies Implemented

Literacy—providing proof for answers

Resources

Online		Streaming
X Resources	___ Video Production	___ Video
	Multimedia	
___ PowerPoint	___ Software	___ Scanner
	Inspiration /	Other:
___ Word	___ Kidspiration	**X** Books
		Other: En-
___ Excel	___ Digital Cameras	**X** cyclopedia
Blog /	Digital Video	
Wiki	**X** Cameras	___ Other:

Library Media Specialist Will:

✦ Guide the students through the Big6 process in locating the information for their projects.

✦ Assist students while they are using the library resources.

✦ Assess the research journals students use to track their research process.

Evaluation

Teacher and library media specialist will take time to debrief the project and adjust as needed for next year.

Attach any other handouts, notes, or materials created for the project.

Figure 4.5 Sample collaboration lesson with primary teacher.

Collaboration Log © 2008, Carl A. Harvey II—http://www.carl-harvey.com. Standards above are excerpted from *Standards for the 21st-Century Learner* by the American Association of School Librarians, a division of the American Library Association, copyright © 2007 American Library Association. Reprinted with permission.

LIBRARY MEDIA CENTER
COLLABORATION PLANNING AND TEACHING LOG

Teacher(s): _____

Grade Level: _____ Intermediate Grades_____ Planning Date: _____ Project Date:_____

Standards for 21st Century Learner	Project Description
1. Inquire, think critically, and gain knowledge. a. Skills: _____1.1.1, 1.1.4, 1.1.3, 1.1.8_____ b. Dispositions: _____1.2.1_____ c. Responsibilities: _____1.3.1, 1.3.5_____ d. Self-Assessment: ___1.4.2_____ **2. Draw conclusions, make informed decisions, apply knowledge to new situations, and create new knowledge.** a. Skills: _____2.1.2, 2.1.4_____ b. Dispositions: _____ c. Responsibilities: _____2.3.1_____ d. Self-Assessment: _____2.4.1_____ **3. Share knowledge and participate ethically and productively as members of our democratic society.** a. Skills: _____3.1.1, 3.1.3_____ b. Dispositions: _____3.2.3_____ c. Responsibilities: _____3.3.4_____ d. Self-Assessment: _____3.4.2_____ **4. Pursue personal and aesthetic growth.** a. Skills: _____ b. Dispositions: _____ c. Responsibilities: _____ d. Self-Assessment: _____	✦ Students are going to an overnight trip to the state capital. They are responsible for planning all the details of the trip. ✦ Students will brainstorm what task need to be completed to be ready for the trip. ✦ They have to provide choices for travel, lodging, activities, meals, etc. Justification will be important, and the class (along with the teacher's guidance) will make the final choices. Timeline: ✦ Students will spend a day brainstorming tasks to complete. ✦ Students will work on search strategies to locate the needed information. They'll need at least a couple of visits to the library media center to locate what they need. ✦ Students will create a presentation to the class about what they found so that decisions can be made.
Academic Standards Math, social studies	**Teacher Will:** ✦ Provide background knowledge and help the students brainstorm the list of tasks to complete. ✦ Provide support to the students during their research. ✦ Co-assess the video and research materials with the library media specialist.
School Improvement **Goals Supported / Strategies Implemented** Mathematics	
Resources <u>X</u> Online Resources __ Video Production Multimedia __ Streaming Video __ PowerPoint __ Software Inspiration / Kidspiration __ Scanner __ Word __ Other: __ Excel __ Digital Cameras __ Other: __ Blog / Wiki __ Digital Video Cameras __ Other:	**Library Media Specialist Will:** ✦ Guide the students through the Big6 to research the information they need. ✦ Help guide them on Web searches to learn how to find what they need efficiently and effectively. ✦ Co-assess the video and research materials with the teacher.
Evaluation	
Teacher and library media specialist will take time to debrief the project and adjust as needed for next year.	

Attach any other handouts, notes, or materials created for the project.

Figure 4.6 Sample collaboration lesson with intermediate teacher.

Collaboration Log © 2008, Carl A. Harvey II—http://www.carl-harvey.com. Standards above are excerpted from *Standards for the 21st-Century Learner* by the American Association of School Librarians, a division of the American Library Association, copyright © 2007 American Library Association. Reprinted with permission.

Assessment

The library media specialist's role in assessment has been growing in recent years. It seems logical that if the skills and information library media specialists teach are important, they should also be assessed. This does not necessarily mean students need a library grade but rather that, as part of a project, there should be assessment of the process and the work students did while working with the library media specialist. Just as the planning and teaching should be collaborative, so should the assessment (Harada and Yoshina 5–6).

Be upfront with students that they will be required to turn in materials that support their work during the project. Students could turn in a journal detailing notes of what they did each day. It could be a flow chart that shows their process—both successes and failures. It could be all the rough drafts, note cards, bibliographies, and so forth. Whatever it is, the documentation should be sufficient to determine if the student was learning the skills needed. See Figure 4.7 for some sample assessments. All of the work done throughout the project should be assessed, and part of the final project grade should reflect the process as well as final product. The library media specialist and classroom teacher may want to do all the assessment together or they may consider dividing up pieces and parts of the project for each to take a role in grading. For example, the library media specialist might assess the research piece while the classroom teacher assesses the final project.

Students need feedback throughout their project. Knowledge of results is motivating. The feedback should be timely and specific (Harada and Yoshina 5). They need to know they are on the right path or that they need to adjust what they are doing. To be successful, everyone needs to know how they are doing, and assessing student work provides students with that feedback. In addition, educators need to know whether the methods are working. If students miss something, then it is important to reteach the skill. If library media specialists are not assessing what the students are learning, how does one know if students are understanding, if they need more support, or if the skill needs to be retaught to the entire class?

Assessment is an important piece of the puzzle because it provides data that helps to tell the story of the library media program. The story it tells is about the learning going on in the library media center. It is important to collect this data not only to influence what we do with students but also to influence how others view the role of the library media program in the school.

Standardized Tests

Every school across the country has at least one form of a standardized test. These multiple choice and written response tests are how our schools are judged to be effective or not effective according to state and national legislation.

As schools develop their curriculum and instruction, teachers are narrowing in on the standards that will be covered on these yearly exams. They are focused on the areas their students did not succeed in and are looking for ways to make them better. These data points drive the school improvement process because the results have a huge impact on the school.

No matter what one's opinion is about these exams, library media specialists need to be part of the group that analyzes and looks at the test results. Library media specialists should be part of the data team in their building. These data teams are not only looking at the test data but also making programmatic decisions that could affect the library media program. If the library

SELF-ASSESSMENT

On what part of your project do you think you did a good job?

What did you think you could have done better?

What was the hardest part of this project?

What was the best place you found information (give a title of a book or the URL of a Web site)

What did you already know that was proven to be correct?

What did you think you knew that was proven to be wrong?

TEACHER ASSESSMENT

Checklist	Yes	No
The student wrote out the task.		
The student created a list of "I wonder . . ." questions.		
The student listed potential places to find information		
The student looked in more than one place for information.		
The student recorded all the information (title, author, etc.) about his/her sources.		
The student used reliable and accurate resources for his/her project.		
The students took notes from his/her sources. Notes were written on index cards.		
The student recorded one fact per card.		
The student used his/her own words when taking notes.		
The student found the answers to their "I wonder . . ." questions.		
The student filed notes into category envelopes.		
The student wrote his or her final project in the synthesis box.		
The student completely answered all of the evaluation questions.		
The student avoided "I don't know, everything, or nothing" when answering the evaluation questions.		
Total Points Earned		

Figure 4.7 Sample assessments.

media specialist is at the table during these discussions, he or she can offer input and suggestions as the school determines how to move forward.

Being aware of the testing data is also an important collaboration tool. When working with teachers, library media specialists should be able to suggest ways through their collaborative projects that they can integrate the skills the students need for the standardized test. As the pressure mounts, teachers often begin to back away from projects because they believe that they are too labor intensive. The teacher will comment they don't have time because they have to prepare for the test. The library media specialist's role is to help teachers see how they can still prepare for the test while using a project-based method instead.

For example, take a written response type question where students have to read a nonfiction passage and then write a response. Those questions are looking for the student to pull information from the passage to support their writing. The library media specialist already knows because of the data analysis that this is an area in which students in her building need additional support. So the library media specialist uses this as an opportunity to help the 4th-grade teacher design a project where students are going to practice strategies for reading informational text. She used her knowledge of the data as an opening to working with the teacher.

The students choose, from a cart of new books, any informational book about animals they wish. The teacher chose this topic because they are currently studying about animals in a variety of biomes. The students then have to read their books and write book reviews. They have to support their opinions of the book by pulling out information and examples from the text. They have to evaluate if the information in the book is accurate, perhaps even cross checking the information in another source.

The activity serves the purpose or practicing the skill for the test but at the same time does it in such a way as to keep the students engaged and connected to the classroom. The library media specialist has taken the lead in helping to model using informational text strategies as well as helping prepare the students for their standardized test.

Beyond the Core Content

Library media specialists often work with the core content subjects such as language arts, math, social studies, and science. Library media specialists gravitate to these areas because they are what are taught in the classroom. The resources in the library media center are heavily focused on the content standards and subjects. However, what about the other areas that are taught in the school?

Related Arts

Related arts could include art, music, physical education, counseling, foreign language, technology, or any subject that is in the rotation that provides teacher release time. Often the library media program is also included in these related arts if the library is on a fixed schedule. The related arts teachers can often be a good place to collaborate.

Consider the music class that is studying composers. Students could research a composer and then create a game based on the information they found to teach the others students in their class about the composers. Student must create a game from scratch. They can base it on Monopoly or CandyLand or any type of board game that students can play. The game focuses on determining why the composer was important, and by the end of the game all the participants should know the composer's contribution.

On a flexible schedule, the library media specialist could attend music class to work with students, or on a fixed schedule, the project could be scheduled so students research their composers during both their music and their library special time. Related arts teachers who experience the benefits of a flexible schedule library media program can become staunch advocates for keeping the library media specialist out of the rotation. See Figures 4.8–4.13 for examples of projects library media specialist might try (or adapt) with related arts teachers.

Each related arts teacher has standards to cover, so creating the opportunity to work with them can open doors to collaboration. Reaching out the hand to offer help and collaboration can build a bridge that creates an ardent supporter of the library media program.

Special Education

Differentiating instruction is a challenging goal. Special education teachers are experts at taking grade level content and presenting it to students at the appropriate level of difficulty. For example, one day the library media specialist suggested doing a research project with the special needs students in a particular grade level. The content taught was the same as the classroom content, but the resources and final product were modified to meet the students' needs. Once the project was over, the special education teacher commented that in all her years of teaching, she had never had a library media specialist offer to work with her kids. She loved it. Now the team regularly plans together for other opportunities for the students to work in the library media center.

As a media specialist builds a library media collection, there is always focus on trying to find several resources at multiple reading levels. It would seem an obvious connection to work with the special education teachers to make sure they know these resources are available and to take that one step further and plan lessons and projects. See Figure 4.14 for a sample project.

As part of school reform and changes in special education law, schools are now putting into place the response to intervention (RTI) process. When concerns about a student begin, this process is how the team walks through determining if or when a child might be tested for special education. The process relies heavily on tracking data of all the interventions tried with the child. If the interventions were successful, the child continues down that path. If they were not successful, new interventions are implemented. The student's progress is monitored on a regular basis to determine the success of the interventions. The results then guide the team on whether to recommend testing.

The RTI team is made up of general education and special education teachers. The team meets to discuss ideas of possible interventions to try and works to be creative in maximizing resources and personnel to help students. The library media specialist may or may not be on the team, but an understanding of the process is important. The library media specialist can be ready to provide resources and support for teachers and students going through the RTI process.

LIBRARY MEDIA CENTER
COLLABORATION PLANNING AND TEACHING LOG

Teacher(s): _____ Music _____

Grade Level: _____ 3rd, 4th or 5th _____ Planning Date: _____ Project Date: _____

Standards for the 21st-Century Learner

1. **Inquire, think critically, and gain knowledge.**
   a. Skills: _____1.1.1, 1.1.4, 1.1.5, 1.1.6_____
   b. Dispositions: _____1.2.3____
   c. Responsibilities: _____1.3.1, 1.3.3, 1.3.5_____
   d. Self-Assessment: ____1.4.4_____

2. **Draw conclusions, make informed decisions, apply knowledge to new situations, and create new knowledge.**
   a. Skills: _____2.1.2, 2.1.4_____
   b. Dispositions: _____2.2.4_____
   c. Responsibilities: _____
   d. Self-Assessment: _____

3. **Share knowledge and participate ethically and productively as members of our democratic society.**
   a. Skills: _____3.1.1, 3.1.3, 3.1.6_____
   b. Dispositions: _____3.2.2_____
   c. Responsibilities: _____
   d. Self-Assessment: _____

4. **Pursue personal and aesthetic growth.**
   a. Skills: _____4.1.1_____
   b. Dispositions: _____
   c. Responsibilities: _____
   d. Self-Assessment: _____

Academic Standards

Music appreciation
English/language arts

School Improvement
Goals Supported / Strategies Implemented

Literacy—writing and informational text

Resources

X Online Resources	___ Video Production Multimedia	___ Streaming Video
___ PowerPoint	___ Software Inspiration /	___ Scanner Other:
___ Word	___ Kidspiration	**X** Books Other:
___ Excel	___ Digital Cameras	**X** Encyclopedia
Blog / **X** Wiki	Digital Video Cameras	___ Other:

Project Description

✦ Students will listen to a variety of musical selections. They will choose the one they like the best.
✦ Students will discover who wrote the piece and complete a research project about that composer.
✦ Students will need to get the normal facts about the composer but also locate any information about why or for whom the piece was written.
✦ Students will write a blog post sharing information about their composer and including their opinions about why they like that particular piece of music.
✦ Students will appropriately reply and correspond using the comments on the blog.

Timeline:

✦ Students will select composer.
✦ Students will research composer and piece of music (two or three days).
✦ Students will compose their blog entry (one or two days).
✦ Students will post to the blog and spend a week interacting, commenting, and discussing.

Teacher Will:

✦ Play a selection from each composer for students to use to select who they are going to research.
✦ Assist students with researching and writing their posts.
✦ Co-assess the final product with library media specialist.

Library Media Specialist Will:

✦ Guide students through the Big6 research process.
✦ Set up the behind-the-scenes stuff for the blog.
✦ Assist students with researching and writing their posts.
✦ Co-assess the final product with the teacher.

Evaluation

Teacher and library media specialist will take time to debrief the project and adjust as needed for next year.

Attach any other handouts, notes, or materials created for the project.

Figure 4.8 Sample collaboration lesson with music specialist.

Collaboration Log © 2008, Carl A. Harvey II—http://www.carl-harvey.com. Standards above are excerpted from *Standards for the 21st-Century Learner* by the American Association of School Librarians, a division of the American Library Association, copyright © 2007 American Library Association. Reprinted with permission.

LIBRARY MEDIA CENTER
COLLABORATION PLANNING AND TEACHING LOG

Teacher(s): _____ Art _____

Grade Level: _____ 2nd Grade_____ Planning Date: _____ Project Date:_____

Standards for the 21st-Century Learner	Project Description
1. Inquire, think critically, and gain knowledge. 　a. Skills: _____ 　b. Dispositions: _____ 　c. Responsibilities: _____ 　d. Self-Assessment: _____ **2. Draw conclusions, make informed decisions, apply knowledge to new situations, and create new knowledge.** 　a. Skills: _____ 　b. Dispositions: _____ 　c. Responsibilities: _____ 　d. Self-Assessment: _____ **3. Share knowledge and participate ethically and productively as members of our democratic society.** 　a. Skills: _____3.1.2, 3.1.3, 3.1.4_____ 　b. Dispositions: _____3.2.3_____ 　c. Responsibilities: _____3.3.2_____ 　d. Self-Assessment: _____ **4. Pursue personal and aesthetic growth.** 　a. Skills: _____4.1.2_____ 　b. Dispositions: _____4.2.4_____ 　c. Responsibilities: _____4.3.1_____ 　d. Self-Assessment: _____	Project would be done during the months of November and December. ✦ Students will evaluate new picture books as potential candidates for the Caldecott Medal. ✦ Classes will work together to create a rubric to evaluate the books and learn how to post to the wiki. ✦ Each student will choose one book about which to write a review and summary. Students will post their reviews on the wiki. Students will then trade books around to read. They will add their comments to the wiki. ✦ Students will work on them as they finish projects early in art, during recess, or at home if they like. If possible, it might be a collaborative project to include the classroom teacher as well. ✦ At the beginning of January, students will vote on the book they think will win the Caldecott Medal. Then they can watch the live announcement of the winner from the ALA Midwinter Conference to see if they were right.
Academic Standards Art appreciation English/language arts	**Teacher will:** ✦ Introduce students to criteria for excellent artwork. ✦ With the library media specialist lead a discussion to create a rubric to assess the books. ✦ Direct students to work on the rating of books as they have extra time in the art room, classroom, or at home.
School Improvement **Goals Supported / Strategies Implemented** Literacy	
Resources 　　Online　　　　　　　　Streaming ___ Resources　___ Video Production　___ Video 　　　　　　　　Multimedia ___ PowerPoint　___ Software　　___ Scanner 　　　　　　Inspiration / ___ Word　　___ Kidspiration　**X** Other: Books ___ Excel　　___ Digital Cameras　___ Other: 　　　　　　Digital Video **X** Blog / Wiki　___ Cameras　___ Other:	**Library Media Specialist will:** ✦ Introduce students to the Caldecott Medal including the criteria for selection. ✦ Send new books to the art room as they come in for the students to rate. ✦ Show the students how to enter their ratings on the wiki. ✦ With the art teacher lead a discussion to create a rubric to assess the books. ✦ Hold the mock election in the library media center in January.
Evaluation	
Teacher and library media specialist will take time to debrief the project and adjust as needed for next year.	

Attach any other handouts, notes, or materials created for the project.

Figure 4.9　Sample collaboration lesson with art specialist.

LIBRARY MEDIA CENTER
COLLABORATION PLANNING AND TEACHING LOG

Teacher(s): _____ P.E _____

Grade Level: _____ 4th or 5th Grade_____ Planning Date: _____ Project Date:_____

Standards for the 21st-Century Learner	Project Description

Standards for the 21st-Century Learner

1. **Inquire, think critically, and gain knowledge.**
   a. Skills: _____1.1.1, _____
   b. Dispositions: _____
   c. Responsibilities: _____
   d. Self-Assessment: _____

2. **Draw conclusions, make informed decisions, apply knowledge to new situations, and create new knowledge.**
   a. Skills: _____2.1.1, 2.1.2, _____
   b. Dispositions: _____
   c. Responsibilities: _____
   d. Self-Assessment: _____

3. **Share knowledge and participate ethically and productively as members of our democratic society.**
   a. Skills: _____3.1.1_____
   b. Dispositions: _____
   c. Responsibilities: _____
   d. Self-Assessment: _____

4. **Pursue personal and aesthetic growth.**
   a. Skills: _____
   b. Dispositions: _____
   c. Responsibilities: _____
   d. Self-Assessment: _____

Project Description

✦ Students determine a list of potential activities they think are good examples of exercise.

✦ As a learning club, students will select one exercise to do research and collect data about.

✦ Students will do some research to see what they can find about the benefits or negatives aspects of the various exercises.

✦ As a learning club, students will determine how they could collect data about their exercise to see if it is helpful.

✦ Students can use spreadsheets to record their data.

✦ Students will report their results by making a commercial to advocate for people to use or not use the exercise.

Timeline:

✦ Students will spend two to three classes deciding on their exercise, research, and data collection.

✦ Students will spend a class writing their commercials and one final class to film it.

Academic Standards

Health/wellness
English/language arts

School Improvement
Goals Supported / Strategies Implemented

Literacy

Teacher Will:

✦ Guide students in brainstorming a list of exercises.

✦ Help them find research information.

✦ Help them determine a data collection method.

✦ Assess the final product.

Resources

___ Online Resources	**X** Video Production Multimedia	___ Streaming Video
___ PowerPoint	___ Software Inspiration / Kidspiration	___ Scanner
___ Word	___ Digital Cameras	___ Other:
X Excel	___ Digital Video	___ Other:
___ Blog / Wiki	**X** Cameras	___ Other:

Library Media Specialist Will:

✦ Help them find research information.

✦ Help them determine a data collection method.

✦ Assess the research and data components.

Evaluation

Teacher and library media specialist will take time to debrief the project and adjust as needed for next year.

Attach any other handouts, notes, or materials created for the project.

Figure 4.10 Sample collaboration lesson with physical education specialist.

LIBRARY MEDIA CENTER
COLLABORATION PLANNING AND TEACHING LOG

Teacher(s): _____ Counselor _____

Grade Level: _____ Planning Date: _____ Project Date: _____

Standards for the 21st-Century Learner

1. **Inquire, think critically, and gain knowledge.**
   a. Skills: _____
   b. Dispositions: _____
   c. Responsibilities: _____
   d. Self-Assessment: _____

2. **Draw conclusions, make informed decisions, apply knowledge to new situations, and create new knowledge.**
   a. Skills: _____
   b. Dispositions: _____
   c. Responsibilities: _____
   d. Self-Assessment: _____

3. **Share knowledge and participate ethically and productively as members of our democratic society.**
   a. Skills: _____
   b. Dispositions: _____
   c. Responsibilities: _____
   d. Self-Assessment: _____

4. **Pursue personal and aesthetic growth.**
   a. Skills: _____ 4.1.1, 4.1.2, 4.1.5 _____
   b. Dispositions: _____
   c. Responsibilities: _____
   d. Self-Assessment: _____

Project Description

✦ Students will brainstorm a list of children's book (picture book) characters.

✦ Students will locate the books and read them in groups of two or three. Then they will reread them, looking for traits and qualities about their character.

✦ Based on their list of traits and what they read they need to decide if the character would be a good friend or not.

✦ Students will report to the group in a community circle discussion.

Academic Standards

Health/wellness—soical skills

School Improvement
Goals Supported / Strategies Implemented

Literacy

Teacher Will:

✦ Talks about the traits of friends.

✦ Help brainstorm a list of characters with the students.

✦ Provide guidance as students decide if their character would be a good friend or not.

Resources

___ Online Resources	___ Video Production Multimedia	___ Streaming Video
___ PowerPoint	___ Software	___ Scanner
___ Word	___ Inspiration / Kidspiration	**X** Books Other:
___ Excel	___ Digital Cameras	___ Other:
___ Blog / Wiki	___ Digital Video Cameras	___ Other:

Library Media Specialist Will:

✦ Talk about the traits of friends.

✦ Help brainstorm a list of characters with the students.

✦ Provide guidance as students decide if their character would be a good friend or not

Evaluation

Teacher and library media specialist will take time to debrief the project and adjust as needed for next year.

Attach any other handouts, notes, or materials created for the project.

Figure 4.11 Sample collaboration lesson with counselor.

LIBRARY MEDIA CENTER
COLLABORATION PLANNING AND TEACHING LOG

Teacher(s): _____ Foreign Language Teacher _____

Grade Level: _____ Planning Date: _____ Project Date:_____

Standards for the 21st-Century Learner

1. Inquire, think critically, and gain knowledge.
   a. Skills: _____ 1.1.1, 1.1.3, 1.1.6, _____
   b. Dispositions: _____
   c. Responsibilities: _____ 1.3.1, _____
   d. Self-Assessment: _____ 1.4.4._____

2. Draw conclusions, make informed decisions, apply knowledge to new situations, and create new knowledge.
   a. Skills: _____ 2.1.2, 2.1.3, _____
   b. Dispositions: _____
   c. Responsibilities: _____
   d. Self-Assessment: _____

3. Share knowledge and participate ethically and productively as members of our democratic society.
   a. Skills: _____ 3.1.1, 3.1.3, 3.1.4, _____
   b. Dispositions: _____
   c. Responsibilities: _____
   d. Self-Assessment: _____

4. Pursue personal and aesthetic growth.
   a. Skills: _____
   b. Dispositions: _____
   c. Responsibilities: _____
   d. Self-Assessment: _____

Project Description

✦ Students will research the culture of the countries where the foreign language is spoken.

✦ Students will look to discover things about that culture's food, entertainment, history, etc.

✦ Students will work together to create a wiki that includes all the information they've located. Then they will work to compare/contrast at least two of the countries. What elements are the same? What are different? Why do you think the two countries speak the same language? Students will use the wiki to post their comments and thoughts.

Timeline:

✦ Two or three class times to research.

✦ Two or three class times to update and post to the wiki.

Academic Standards

Foreign language
Social studies

School Improvement
Goals Supported / Strategies Implemented

Literacy

Resources

	Online	Streaming
X Resources	Video Production	___ Video
	Multimedia	
___ PowerPoint	___ Software	___ Scanner
	Inspiration /	
___ Word	___ Kidspiration	___ Other:
___ Excel	___ Digital Cameras	___ Other:
	Digital Video	
X Blog / Wiki	___ Cameras	___ Other:

Teacher Will:

✦ Help the student discover what countries speak the language they are studying.

✦ Assist students with research.

✦ Assist students in creating their wiki.

✦ Co-assess the project with the library media specialist.

Library Media Specialist Will:

✦ Help the student discover what countries speak the language they are studying.

✦ Guide students with the Big6 research process.

✦ Assist students in creating their wiki.

✦ Co-assess the project with the teacher.

Evaluation

Teacher and library media specialist will take time to debrief the project and adjust as needed for next year.

Attach any other handouts, notes, or materials created for the project.

Figure 4.12 Sample collaboration lesson with foreign language specialist.

Teacher(s): _____ Computer Lab Teacher_____

Grade Level: _____ Planning Date: _____ Project Date:_____

Standards for the 21st-Century Learner	**Project Description**

Standards for the 21st-Century Learner

1. **Inquire, think critically, and gain knowledge.**
   a. Skills: _____ 1.1.5_____
   b. Dispositions: _____
   c. Responsibilities: _____
   d. Self-Assessment: _____

2. **Draw conclusions, make informed decisions, apply knowledge to new situations, and create new knowledge.**
   a. Skills: _____
   b. Dispositions: _____
   c. Responsibilities: _____
   d. Self-Assessment: _____

3. **Share knowledge and participate ethically and productively as members of our democratic society.**
   a. Skills: _____
   b. Dispositions: _____
   c. Responsibilities: _____
   d. Self-Assessment: _____

4. **Pursue personal and aesthetic growth.**
   a. Skills: _____
   b. Dispositions: _____
   c. Responsibilities: _____
   d. Self-Assessment: _____

Project Description

✦ Students will visit Web sites that are bogus and contain incorrect information but appear to be completely true.

✦ Students will be tested to see if they can notice the inconsistency.

✦ Students will then create an evaluation tool to help them as they begin a research project that is coming up.

Academic Standards

English/language arts—research skills

**School Improvement
Goals Supported / Strategies Implemented**

Literacy

Resources

X	Online Resources	___	Video Production	___	Streaming Video
___	PowerPoint	___	Multimedia Software	___	Scanner
___	Word	___	Inspiration / Kidspiration	___	Other:
___	Excel	___	Digital Cameras	___	Other:
___	Blog / Wiki	___	Digital Video Cameras	___	Other:

Teacher Will:

✦ Help students create a guide for evaluating Web sites.

✦ Look for bogus sites to share with students.

Library Media Specialist Will:

✦ Help students create a guide for evaluating Web sites.

✦ Look for bogus sites to share with students.

✦ Discuss and demonstrate implications of including information that is wrong in projects.

Evaluation

Teacher and library media specialist will take time to debrief the project and adjust as needed for next year.

Attach any other handouts, notes, or materials created for the project.

Figure 4.13   Sample collaboration lesson with technology specialist.

LIBRARY MEDIA CENTER
COLLABORATION PLANNING AND TEACHING LOG

Teacher(s): _____Special Education_____

Grade Level: _____Primary_____ Planning Date: _____ Project Date:_____

Standards for the 21st-Century Learner	**Project Description**

Standards for the 21st-Century Learner

1. **Inquire, think critically, and gain knowledge.**
   a. Skills: _____ 1.1.1, 1.1.3, 1.1.4, 1.1.6_____
   b. Dispositions: _____1.2.1, 1.2.6_____
   c. Responsibilities: _____1.3.1, 1.3.5_____
   d. Self-Assessment: _____1.4.1, 1.4.4_____

2. **Draw conclusions, make informed decisions, apply knowledge to new situations, and create new knowledge.**
   a. Skills: _____
   b. Dispositions: _____
   c. Responsibilities: _____
   d. Self-Assessment: _____

3. **Share knowledge and participate ethically and productively as members of our democratic society.**
   a. Skills: _____
   b. Dispositions: _____
   c. Responsibilities: _____
   d. Self-Assessment: _____

4. **Pursue personal and aesthetic growth.**
   a. Skills: _____
   b. Dispositions: _____
   c. Responsibilities: _____
   d. Self-Assessment: _____

Project Description

✦ Students will locate information about the various forms of weather found in each season (summer, fall, winter, and spring) in Indiana.

✦ Students will use the information to determine what kind of clothes they need to buy to be dressed properly for each season.

✦ Students will make a shopping list. Using an online shopping site, students will record the price for each item and determine the final costs.

Academic Standards

Science
Health

School Improvement
Goals Supported / Strategies Implemented

Literacy

Teacher Will:

✦ Help students read the books to locate facts that will help determine what kind of clothing is needed for each season.

✦ Help students locate prices on shopping Web site.

✦ Help students create their shopping list.

Resources

	Online	Video		Streaming
X	Resources	__	Production	__ Video
			Multimedia	
__	PowerPoint	__	Software	__ Scanner
			Inspiration /	
__	Word	__	Kidspiration	**X** Other: Books
			Digital	
__	Excel	__	Cameras	__ Other:
			Digital Video	
__	Blog / Wiki	__	Cameras	__ Other:

Library Media Specialist Will:

✦ Help students read the books to locate facts that will help determine what kind of clothing is needed for each season.

✦ Help students locate prices on shopping Web site.

✦ Help students create their shopping list.

Evaluation

Teacher and library media specialist will take time to debrief the project and adjust as needed for next year.

Attach any other handouts, notes, or materials created for the project.

Figure 4.14 Sample collaboration lesson with special education specialist.

Collaboration Log © 2008, Carl A. Harvey II—http://www.carl-harvey.com. Standards above are excerpted from *Standards for the 21st-Century Learner* by the American Association of School Librarians, a division of the American Library Association, copyright © 2007 American Library Association. Reprinted with permission.

Library media specialists cannot focus exclusively on the general classroom teacher. The library media specialist has a responsibility to related arts and special education, too. The AASL's *Standards for the 21st Century Learner* and ISTE's *National Educational Technology Standards for Students* apply to all subjects. It is good for students to see those connections outside the core standards.

The library media specialist's job is to teach and work with all students. It means that he has to work with all teachers in the building, too. It can be difficult when personalities clash, but the bottom line is serving the students. The library media specialist and the teachers have to move past any possible differences they might have for the benefits of the students.

One thing that is important about school libraries is they have always been a place where any student can learn. Library media specialists need to be aware of how students are identified, what support resources they need available to them, and, by working with the special education teachers, how the library media program can have an impact for all students in the building.

ELL

English language learners (ELLs) are another growing population in many schools across the country. ELL students are students who need additional language support. Perhaps they moved to this country and do not know English, or perhaps English is not spoken at home, so they need additional practice and support. The library media center can be another place for these students to feel that they are a part of the school. It can be a place where they feel they are successful.

It will be important to work with the ELL teachers to determine how the library media program can be supportive. The library media center might need to expand its collection of bilingual resources to support struggling ELL readers. The library media specialist may need to help classroom teachers adapt and modify projects for ELL students. Materials at a variety of levels on a variety of topics will be important so that ELL students can be successful while working in the library media center, too.

Either special education or ELL requires the library media specialist to be aware of the students in their building. They need to talk with teachers about the needs and issues the children they are working with have. This will allow the library media specialist to better focus on working with those children and meeting their needs.

Instruction Organization

As collaboration becomes the norm in the school, develop a yearlong plan for the library media center to map out the units and instruction. Use the collaboration log to help develop the plan so that it includes both big projects and those that are maybe just one lesson or two. See Figure 4.15 for a sample chart. Use Excel or Word to make it easy to update and change as the year progresses. It also can help the library media specialist to track busier times of the year. The library media specialist may want to try to stagger bigger projects so that multiple grade levels are not all involved in large projects all at once. Also consider the gradual release of responsibility. As teachers begin to feel more comfortable with units and projects, they can

Month:

	Week 1	Week 2	Week 3	Week 4
Kindergarten	Topics / Unit Themes			
1st Grade				
2nd Grade				
3rd Grade				
4th Grade				
Special Areas, Special Education, High Ability, etc.				

Figure 4.15 Sample yearlong plan.

take the lead so that the library media specialist can focus on new projects. The library media specialist is sill there to offer support, but the teacher begins to take the lead.

Wiki Wrap-Up

Library media specialists have seen their job evolve over the decades. The role library media specialists play with curriculum—planning, teaching, and assessing—has grown dramatically. Library media specialists play a pivotal role in preparing students for the 21st century. For additional resources, check out the companion wiki Web site (http://www.carl-harvey.com/librarytieswiki/).

Works Cited

American Association of School Librarians. *Empowering Learners: Guidelines for School Library Media Programs.* Chicago: American Association of School Librarians, 2009.

American Association of School Librarians. *Standards for the 21st Century Learner.* Chicago: American Association of School Librarians, 2007.

American Association of School Librarians. *Standards for the 21st Century Learner in Action.* Chicago: American Association of School Librarians, 2009.

American Association of School Librarians and Association for Educational Communications and Technology. *Information Power.* Chicago: American Library Association, 1988. Reprint 1998.

Buzzeo, Toni. *The Collaboration Handbook.* Columbus, OH: Linworth Publishing, 2008.

Harada, Violet H. and Joan M. Yoshina. *Assessing Learning: Librarians and Teachers as Partners.* Westport, CT: Libraries Unlimited, 2005.

International Society for Technology in Education. *National Educational Technology Standards for Students* (2nd ed.). Eugene, OR: International Society for Technology in Education, 2007.

Loertscher, David V. *Taxonomies of the School Library Media Program* (2nd ed.). San Jose, CA: Hi Willow Research and Publishing, 2000.

CHAPTER 5

Programming

Engaging students and faculty in the school library includes library media specialist created programs that will entice them to use the library space and its collection.

—Marla W. McGhee and Barbara A. Jansen, *The Principal's Guide to a Powerful Library Media Program*

Beyond instruction, the library media program also offers programming to students and staff. The library media specialist designs programming to motivate students to read, to interact with technology, to come to the library media center, and so forth. These additional connections can create lasting memories for students that give them a positive feeling about the library media center. Programs are also some of the ways to get word out into the community about the positive happenings in the school library media center.

Promoting Reading

The first common belief in the new American Association of School Librarians (AASL) *Standards for the 21st Century Learner* talks about reading. In the 21st century, reading remains a primary function of the library media program. However, the different types of resources available for students are changing. From e-books, to Playaways, to downloaded audiobooks, there are all kinds of electronic resources in the collections to help readers succeed.

Electronic programs such as Accelerated Reader and Scholastic Reading Counts became popular as computers moved into the library media centers. They continue to be very popular, but questions remain about their effectiveness. As technology has advanced, there are many other avenues to track and assess what students read for pleasure. Automation systems such as Follett's Destiny allow users to write book reviews that are added to the MARC records (much like Amazon.com). Also, videos and audio multimedia can be added as well. Student course systems such as Moodle—an open source program that allows students to login to access resources and activities for a course—provide a forum where children can discuss various books they have read. The easy to use FlipVideo cameras are a great way that young readers could make short Reading Rainbow segments to share on the Web or the televised morning announcements show.

Library catalogs also have become a way to promote reading. Many automation systems also have the option to include images of the book jackets in the catalog. Most offer this for an additional fee but it can be very helpful in an elementary school. Students who are sure they won't check out a book quickly change their tune, sometimes when they see the cover of the book on the screen.

The catalog can also have features like a list of the top 10 most checked out items as well as teacher recommended lists. Students and staff can also create and add book reviews in print, audio, and video formats to share with other students. Students and staff can create recommended lists and recommend titles to others. Library Web pages now have the ability to post podcasts, videos, and other resources online to promote reading. Moodle, blogs, or wikis have become a great way to facilitate an online book discussion. See Appendix B for examples of these tools used in schools.

However, library media programs go beyond just promoting reading. Today in elementary library media centers, library media specialists are teaching students how to read. When reading stories and text, we're modeling comprehension strategies. Library media specialists are demonstrating a variety of language arts skills and strategies with each page they read. A good example of these connections can be seen in a matrix between reading comprehension strategies and AASL's *Standards for the 21st Century Learner* developed by Judi Morellion(http://storytrail.com/Impact/matrix.htm).

Libraries can offer a lot more than just story time anymore. Every activity and lesson we plan, teach, and assess needs to be rooted in sound instructional practice. How can we transform simply reading the story into a discussion about fluency, comprehension, phonics, and so forth? This certainly is not to say that reading for pleasure doesn't have its place in the library media center, but it does mean that the library media specialist should be deliberate in his or her choices.

The library media specialist's role in teaching reading has also added to the turf wars in some buildings. Beyond battles with technology, there can also be issues with literacy coaches. Again, there can be overlap between the two positions, but at the same time there is great opportunity for becoming collaborative partners. Think of the projects, activities, and resources the two leaders in a building could put together if they worked as a team.

Finally, one of the easiest ways to promote reading is to evaluate the policies in the library media centers. Are there policies that prevent children from getting access to materials? What are the reasons? Do they outweigh the benefits?

In Chapter 7, the topic of policies will be more defined, but in this section it is enough to note that our policies can have a huge impact on student reading habits. Consider the library where students come once a week to check out materials, are limited to two items, and don't come back to the library media center for another week. The student takes the books home and reads them that night, but they remain in his desk the rest of the week until it is time to go back to the library. Now, think about the school where students come to the library media center and check out books. They can check out an unlimited number of books; however, they have a discussion about being responsible users. The student opts to check out three books. She takes them home, reads them, and brings them back to school the next day when she can go to the library again for more. Now, which student is going to have more access to reading materials? How do the policies we have affect the promotion of reading? Consider the policies in your library media center now. What could be changed to increase student use and interest?

Young Author's Celebration

Celebrating student writing is important. Annually students prepare one piece of writing that they take through the entire writing process all the way to publishing. This writing is then displayed and shared during a young author's celebration. Students are encouraged to donate writing to the library media center for others to read and enjoy as well.

Some school libraries have a special appropriately decorated "author's chair" where students sign up with the media specialist to sit and read a work written by the student.

Moving beyond printing out these books, students could use a wiki or a Web site as a way to share their writing. Maybe students would borrow FlipVideo cameras to record themselves reading their writing and play those during the celebration. Consider posting these videos to the Internet as well. The Internet and Web 2.0 tools allow students to expand their audience for their writing. Imagine the joy of a grandparent in California who can hear and see his or her grandchild in Virginia reading a story he or she wrote. Be sure to follow district guidelines for posting student work online.

Student Choice State Book Award Programs

Many states have a book award to honor authors and illustrators at various levels. These awards are often given based on the book that receives the most student votes. Committees of various groups (quite often school library media professional organizations) compile a list of nominees and then the students read them and vote on their favorite. Voting day can often be a huge celebration in the library media center. Check out Sharon McElmeel's list of state student book choice awards (http://www.mcelmeel.com/curriculum/bookawards.html)

Extracurricular Clubs
Book Clubs

There are lots of different types of book clubs. There are the traditional clubs where the students read the same book and come together at a set time to discuss it. There are the clubs where students all read books by the same author. Again, they come together at a set time to discuss the books. In elementary schools, lunch times makes a great time to pull groups like this together where students can eat and talk at the same time. Book clubs could be formal where everyone in the class is in a club (especially in older grades this looks very much liked a leveled reading block of time), or they can be more informal, where it is optional for the students.

The social connections of Web 2.0 make it possible to expand beyond meeting at school. Consider conducting a book discussion using a blog. Make sure to research district policies about blogs before starting one. There are any free services available, but they are out on the Internet for all to see. Perhaps a somewhat safer alternative is David Warlick's Class Blogmeister (http://www.classblogmeister.com). Your tech department may also have options for how you can do it internally without students posting to the Internet, so consult with them as well.

Ask for volunteers from the students to be responsible for starting with a question, and the rest of the club then responds to his question. Then another student takes the lead. Follow this pattern until all club members have taken the lead question or until the interest in the book is finished. For younger students, the library media specialist might begin with the opening question.

For a more secure discussion, installing the Moodle course management software provides a more protected environment for students. Here students can have a discussion forum to talk about a book, too. Consider collaboration with other elementary schools in the district to expand the potential pool of kids interacting to discuss book(s).

The book club is more about promoting books in the school, and students can read any book or author of their choosing. Give them choices of making a video or a podcast to promote the book to other students in the school. Upload the images to the library media center Web page, blog, or automation system. Make sure to follow any district policies and procedures about posting student work online.

Another option for a book club is to bring parents and children together to read. Choose a book that appeals to many people on a variety of levels. Use some of the previously mentioned technology options to interact, or perhaps a school-wide celebration at the end of the club would be in order for students and parents to share with each other about the book they read.

Student Assistant Club

Student assistants can provide invaluable help to the library media center. Some schools might call them by a clever name such as Jr. Librarians or The Clickers. Students might help with some of the clerical tasks in the library media center and then also may become the experts on technology to help other students or a teacher. See Chapter 2, under Student Assistants, for a potential list of tasks.

This club could meet before or after school, or students could come to the library media center during recess. Have students apply for the positions at the beginning of the year. They fill out a simple application. See Figure 5.1 for an example of a possible application. One school has two slots each day where six students come to work in the library media center. Any given student comes only once a week. This way students also get their recess most of the week. The club can accommodate up to 60 students. A checklist keeps track of what job students have

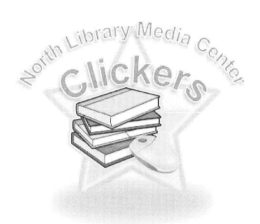

Do you like to help out in the school?
Do you enjoy working with technology?
Do you like looking at and working with all the great books in the library media center?

If you answered yes, apply now to join the North Library Media Center Clickers!

Name: _____

Teacher: _____

Why would you like to join the North Library Media Center Clickers?

What LifeSkills would you use if you were a member of the North Library Media Center Clickers?

Teacher's Signature_____

Figure 5.1 Student assistants application.

	Turn on Lights	Turn on Computers	Writing Center	Research Journals	DIR Tickets Sort (Fri)	Dust / Clean	Trim Lamination	Die Cut Letters	Run Copies	Makes Posters	Load Paper in Printers	Clean Computer Screens	Digital Cameras	Flip Video Cameras	Pull Books for Teachers	Check In/Out Books	Straighten Shelves	Shelve —Enjoyable	Shelve —Fiction	Shelve —Nonfiction	Shelve —Graphic Novels	Shelve —Magazines	Shelve —Biographies	Shelve —Reference	Shelve —Videos	Shelve —Professional	Straighten Puppets
Monday—Lunch																											
Student Name—Room Number																											
Student Name—Room Number																											
Student Name—Room Number																											
Student Name—Room Number																											
Student Name—Room Number																											
Student Name—Room Number																											
Monday—Recess																											
Student Name—Room Number																											
Student Name—Room Number																											
Student Name—Room Number																											
Student Name—Room Number																											
Student Name—Room Number																											
Student Name—Room Number																											
Tuesday—Lunch																											
Student Name—Room Number																											
Student Name—Room Number																											
Student Name—Room Number																											
Student Name—Room Number																											
Student Name—Room Number																											
Student Name—Room Number																											
Tuesday—Recess																											
Student Name—Room Number																											
Student Name—Room Number																											
Student Name—Room Number																											
Student Name—Room Number																											
Student Name—Room Number																											
Student Name—Room Number																											

Figure 5.2 Student assistant training checklist.

learned. This helps make it manageable for the library media staff. See Figure 5.2 for a sample checklist.

Technology Clubs

Technology clubs are a great way to train small groups of students who can in turn support their teachers and fellow students. This club could be folded in with the student assistant club, or it could be a club on its own. Each class would have one or two representatives in the club. The club would focus on a variety of technology tools available in the building—from digital cameras to DVD players to computer software programs.

The student then becomes the expert, so if the teacher has difficulties, the first call is to his or her student technology club member, and then if he or she still needs help he or she can contact the library media specialist or technology support people. This gives the kids some ownership and hopefully cuts down on the time a library media specialist might spend solving some basic problems.

Morning Announcements

A lot of schools have access to equipment to do a morning announcements show over a closed-circuit TV system. Some schools record it and some schools perform it live each day. Students take on the roles of anchors, producers, writers, reporters, directors, teleprompter, and so froth. The crew might be anywhere from 6 to 10 students. Some programs rotate their crew periodically to give more students an opportunity to be a part of the team.

Morning announcements are a great vehicle for students to practice public speaking, working on writing and editing, learning to use a variety of technology equipment, and a good opportunity to promote the library media program, too.

The crew could expand their role to help utilize the studio beyond the morning announcements. Students who have been on the crew can be experts when their classes are using the studio for projects.

Enrichments and Special Programs

The library media program has the opportunity to plan and host wonderful enrichment programs for students.

Author Visits

Author visits are a real-life experience for students and staff. To connect with the authors and illustrators who write the books that line the shelves is a thrill students will remember long after they leave the halls of the school. The typical author visit provides for one to three presentations during the day. The author also will have a book signing where students and staff can get their books autographed. These events become ingrained in the students' memories. Circulation of the visiting author's books remains high for many years.

An author visit creates a shared experience for the entire school. Whenever possible, host the author in the library media center. It is a more intimate setting. One library moves out all of the furniture to make room for entire grade levels to sit on the floor to listen to the author visit.

Bringing authors to the school can be costly. Author visits can cost around $2,000 or more by the time one includes author speaking fees, transportation, and lodging. So how can library media specialists use technology to bring authors into the schools? Projects such as Ball State University's MyVisit—Virtual Author Visits (http://www.bsu.edu/myvisit/index.html) bring authors into the school via the computer or distance learning equipment. Author Toni Buzzeo has a list of authors on her Web site who are willing to do various types of electronic connection visits. Check her list at (http://www.tonibuzzeo.com/visitvirtual.html). While these may not be free, the fees might be less expensive than bringing the author to the school to visit face-to-face. There are many tools like AOL Instant Messenger, Skype, and so forth that provide a format for connecting electronically with minimal technology costs.

After-School Programs

Bring students into the library media center after school to celebrate reading. At one school an after-school program is a way to motivate student to read books from the state student choice award. Students all read the same book and then stay after school for a program where there are activities and food based on the book they read.

Beyond the school day, the library media center can also offer support for tutoring. Look for opportunities for funding to keep the library media center open after school (or before school) for tutoring. Can you get volunteers or teachers to help offer support for students? It will be important to make sure transportation is also available for students who stay late whether such transportation is provided by the school district or whether parents need to arrange other opportunities.

What about when students are in the midst of big projects? Can the library media center be open in the evenings for parents and students to use? Can grant funds be found to pay for staff to stay and keep the facility available in the evening? Is there a way to adjust hours of support staff to cover evening hours? The library media specialist needs to work with administrators to look for creative ways to fund and offer services to students.

Gaming

Gaming in libraries has been another hook to bring students into the library media center. From board games to electronic games, libraries are offering programming. Christopher Harris and the member librarians of the Genesee Valley BOCES in New York have created an alignment of a variety of games with the *Standards for the 21st Century Learner.* Check out their Web site for the alignment and other gaming resources (http://sls.gvboces.org/gaming/)

Gaming could be special events offered after school or even a lunchtime/recess activity. Many of the games have curricular connections that could be resources for literacy or math stations in the classroom. Gaming is an example of how 21st-century libraries are pulling in students by going to where the students are interested.

Wiki Wrap-Up

Years after they leave the school, students are not going to remember a worksheet they filled out or a test they took. Create those learning opportunities that are unique and meaningful, and students will remember them for a lifetime. They'll have a positive response any time someone begins to talk about school libraries. For additional resources, check out the companion wiki Web site (http://www.carl-harvey.com/librarytieswiki/).

Works Cited

American Association of School Librarians. *Standards for the 21st Century Learner.* Chicago: American Association of School Librarians, 2007.

CHAPTER 6

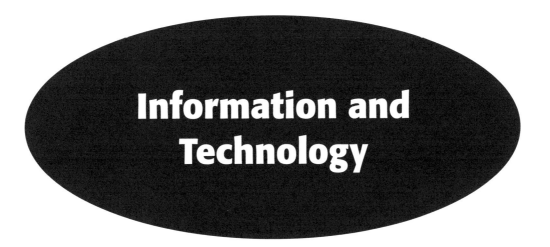

Information and Technology

Educators should seek to integrate literacy, rather than integrate technology. If we rethink what it is to be literate in today's information environment, and integrate that, then the technology will come. But it will not come because we are convinced that laying the children's hands on these machines will make them smarter, or better prepared for their future. Computers and the Internet will be an essential part of teaching and learning because they are the tools of contemporary literacy.

—David F. Warlick, *Redefining Literacy 2.0* (2nd ed.)

Throughout this book there are many references to the technology tools of the 21st century. Technology is such a prevalent component of the 21st-century learning environment that it is appropriate to devote an entire chapter to the topic. However, it is also important to embrace Warlick's quote. Placing the focus on teaching students literacy is the key. Educators need to use information and resources to teach kids how to be literate, and that, in turn, will lead them to the technology (Warlick xii–xiii).

Technology continues to grow at an astronomical rate. Every day there are new applications and tools that students, teachers, and library media specialists can use. It can seem daunting (especially to teachers who did not grow up using computers) to wonder how they can possibly learn how to use all of these resources or keep up as new ones are coming. Educators need to feel comfortable letting the students show them how to use these technology tools and then, in turn, educators can help students learn more effectively and make good decisions on what to do with the technology.

Many of these technology tools were not originally designed to be tools used in education; however, educators and students are finding ways to make these tools part of the educational landscape. Because many of these tools are open for anyone to use, it is sometimes hard to avoid topics or words that might be inappropriate for young elementary students to see or hear. This does not mean the tools do not have value or should not be used with students but rather that one has to be reasonably cautious and more creative in how one can use them with students. Be sure to follow district guidelines. Talk to students about the potential of finding inappropriate things on the Web and what process they should follow if they do.

Technology in Elementary Schools

Defining what technology looks like in a typical elementary school is difficult. Even within the same district the resources available at one school can be different than at another. Budgets often dictate how often equipment is upgraded or when new tools can be purchased. Administrators, teachers, and library media specialists may work on grants or have specific requests for technology that may not be needed in another building. Web 2.0 tools have opened the doors to technology a bit wider. Open source software, software that is usually available free and permits the user to alter or change it for their personal needs, and online tools have made it easier for some buildings to advance with technology even when funding remained limited.

Literacy—being able to read, write, and communicate—dominates instruction and assessments in today's elementary schools. However, as David Warlick suggests, the types of literacy skills students need are changing. Beyond just being able to read, students must think critically to use, evaluate, and then create or repackage their own information. He asserts that technology should not be viewed as something we integrate. It will become a tool of its own because students will need it to be literate (Warlick xiii).

Productivity software is a major component in elementary schools. Software where students can create and share, such as Kidspiration, Microsoft Word and Microsoft PowerPoint, Kid Pix, and so forth, allows students to create information. Open source options like Open Office (http://www.openoffice.org) and Tux Paint (http://www.tuxpaint.org) provide a way for schools to use similar tools at significant cost savings.

In addition to the software programs that can be installed, there are new applications that are totally Web based. These Web 2.0 tools expand the resources that can be used with students. While many of these tools have great appeal, they also come with ads or no restraints on what people can post. This makes it more difficult to use these with elementary students. Wordle (http://www.wordle.net) is a prime example of this. However, work with the technology experts. Perhaps the application can be unblocked, but the gallery of Wordles created by others could still be blocked. This lets students use the tool, but still protect students from inappropriate content.

Teachers Embracing Technology

There are always a few teachers (and library media specialists) who seem to prefer to avoid using technology. Just as library media specialists are teaching students how to use information (and in turn the technology that goes along with accessing information), teachers need to be learners as well. Consider the video on TeacherTube titled "Did You Know? 2.0" (http://www.teachertube.com/viewVideo.php?video_id=3051). These stats provide examples of how the world is changing for today's students. When working with teachers to adopt new technology strategies, here are some things for them to ponder:

Information Is Changing

✦ As the research and knowledge of their content fields grow and evolve, teachers need to be able to adapt and alter their curriculum accordingly. Based on state and national learning standards, curriculum is updated routinely today. Rapidly changing and growing information is changing the way people think and what people know. Teaching must reflect that change.

Students Learn Differently

✦ The lecture classroom of the past is gone. Students need to be able to learn in an environment where they can think, share, and thrive. They need resources and access to information quickly. Mark Prensky says that technology's role is to support students teaching themselves (Prensky 1). Students today are very social and use technology as a means for interacting with one another. Educators should take advantage of those social skills to help students learn, too.

Professional Development

✦ Learning for adults is changing, too. While educators rely on well-researched, authoritative professional books to read, professionals are also using blogs, wikis, podcasts, Web sites, Twitter, and Facebook. All of these and the new emerging resources build up a network of people one can learn from, share with, and in turn, grow professionally. While these items may be blocked at school, educators should consider checking them out from home.

Administrator Support

✦ Today's building administrators expect teachers to use technology. E-mail was a catalyst that brought along a revolution in how educators communicate with each other. Now administrators are using blogs, wikis, and Web sites to share information with teachers, students, parents, and the community. As they evaluate teachers, they will expect to see teachers using technology as an integral part of their instruction, their students' projects, and their assessment.

As library media specialists work with teachers, they can help them see the opportunities of connecting what they are teaching to information sources and technology. Library media specialists can show teachers how their students can be more successful with the resources available. Library media specialists can show teachers how their students have different opportunities and audiences available to them when they use technology.

Today students learn differently than adults do, so in order to be successful, educators are going to have to change strategies. This difference comes from the experience that today's students have had. They grew up with the technology already in place. Therefore their experiences have changed how their brains think (Prensky 1).

Libraries Leading with Technology

Many library media specialists were early adopters of technology and learned as they went. Some embraced these new tools that were brought into the school. They helped both teachers and students begin to use them.

As technology exploded, so did the staffing required to keep it running. Technology departments started appearing in schools everywhere, and in some places a battle began of media versus technology. While the library media specialist was happy to give up the job of fixing broken equipment, the instructional and collaborative role that technology brought was exciting and important. Schools continued to grow with technology, and many schools began to hire technology integration specialists. The integrator's job seemed to overlap with part of the role of the library media specialist, sometimes causing turf battles.

Moving forward, library media specialists and technology integration specialists are all working toward the same goal. The two groups must collaborate to work together. Allison Zmuda and Violet Harada in their book *Librarians as Learning Specialists* suggest that the various learning specialists in the building work together to determine roles and responsibilities for projects. They should communicate with one another to ensure that the best result for students is the outcome.

Automation Systems

Technology advances have also been made in library automation systems. Many systems are now Web-based so that users can access the databases and resources from anywhere. Library media specialists can access the system from home as well as from their office.

Systems are now designed using graphic interfaces, including Amazon-like features such as the ability to add reviews, to recommend resources to other users, and to add video, sound, and images of the book covers. For elementary students, graphical interfaces are helpful. Including options for suggestions when words are misspelled is also helpful. From the library side, being able to do self-checkout with elementary students also frees up the library media specialist or library assistants as well. The catalog has to be useful for students and teachers as well as the library media specialist.

Besides these features, there are several automation systems that are open source software. These systems are gaining in popularity because of their relatively low cost and their customizability.

All of the various companies are evaluating the landscape and noticing the way Web 2.0 is making the Internet more participatory. The library automation vendors are adding many of these same features to their catalogs, too. See Figure 6.1 for a list of automation systems.

Databases

Library media specialists love databases. They love guiding students to resources where they can find trusted information. There are countless databases available for middle school, high school, and beyond. However, there hasn't always been a vast amount of choices for elementary students. The wide range of reading levels in an elementary school makes it harder to create databases that could be used at multiple levels. However, in recent years, the databases available have continued to design interfaces that are more elementary appropriate and add resources at a variety of reading levels. See Figure 6.2 for a list of online databases.

World Book Online (http://www.worldbookonline) has been around for a while, but its creators continue to adapt and improve on their product. Recent advancements provide three different levels and layout designs that are appropriate for students at various times in their school careers.

Alexandria Library Software

    http://www.goalexandria.com

Book Systems

    http://www.booksys.com

Evergreen

    http://open-ils.org

Follett Software Company—Destiny

    http://www.fsc.follett.com

Koha

    http://liblime.com/koha

Library World

    http://www.libraryworld.com

Mandarin Library Automation

    http://www.mlasolutions.com

OPALS

    http://www.mediaflex.net/search_product.jsp?category=A&page_no=1

Sirsi/Dynix

    http://www.sirsidynix.com/Solutions/Markets/school.php

Surpass

    http://www.surpasssoftware.com

The Library Company

    http://www.tlcdelivers.com

Figure 6.1 Library automation systems.

Capstone Publishing—PebbleGo (subscription required)

http://www.capstonepress.com

> This database is designed for students in kindergarten through 2nd grade. It is focused on animals and parallels their Pebble Book series; over 200 animals are listed along with audio and video footage. Includes the ability for the text to be read to students.

Capstone Publishing—Interactive Books (subscription required)

http://capstoneinteractivelibrary.com

> Collections of interactive books online (or CD) that students can either have read to them or they can read on their own. Links to other Web sites are included as well.

EBSCOhost—Kids Search (subscription required)

http://www.ebscohost.com

> Database is designed for elementary and middle grade students. It has a graphical interface for ease of us. Some databases that use the interface also will report back Lexile levels of the text. This interface can be use with several of the EBSCO databases.

EBSCOhost—Searchasaurus (subscription required)

http://www.ebscohost.com

> This is another search interface from EBSCO, but it only works with a select few of their databases. It is enhanced by a dinosaur theme that assists students in developing their searching skills. Results students find are marked with Lexile level of the text.

Gale Cengage—InfoTrac Kid's Edition (subscription required)

http://www.gale.cengage.com

> Designed for students in kindergarten through 6th grade, this databases gives students access to magazines, reference books, and newspapers on a variety of topics.

Gale Cengage—Kids InfoBits (subscription required)

http://www.gale.cengage.com

> Designed for students in kindergarten through 5th grade, this database includes an almanac, information about countries and states, encyclopedia, dictionary, and other information.

International Children's Digital Library Foundation (free)

http://en.childrenslibrary.org

> Filled with children's books all over the world, this database is full of resources for teachers and library media specialists. Books from other cultures from around the world are easily accessible. The library is a good tool for bringing in other perspectives and cultures.

One More Story (subscription required)

http://www.onemorestory.com

> This database contains well over 100 books. The titles are from some of the major publishers and includes full-text of the entire book. Books can be read aloud and include background music as well. Additional activities and resources are also provided.

Figure 6.2 Online elementary databases.

ProQuest—eLibrary elementary (subscription required)

http://www.proquestk12.com/libraryspot.shtml

> This database provides information from a variety of resources—books, magazine, video, audio, and so forth. Material is selected for appropriateness for elementary age students. Students use colorful icons or a variety of search options to locate information.

ProQuest—SIRS Discoverer (subscription required)

http://www.proquestk12.com/libraryspot.shtml

> This is a general reference database for students in grades 1 through 9. All the articles are full-text and thousands of images, charts, maps, and so forth are included.

Scholastic Library—Grolier Online (subscription required)

http://go.grolier.com

> Within Grolier online are a variety of databases including: New Book of Knowledge, Amazing Animals of the World, Lands and People, and so forth. One can pick and choose which databases to include in their subscription.

Scholastic Library—BookFlix (subscription required)

http://teacher.scholastic.com/products/bookflixfreetrial

> BookFlix is an online literacy tool. There are a variety of books—both nonfiction and fiction—that students can read (or that can be read to them) and a variety of activities.

TeachingBooks.net (subscription required)

http://teachingbooks.net

> This database is a one-stop shop for anything to do with authors and books. It includes video author interviews, name pronunciation guide, and access to tons of online resources to support a variety of authors and books.

Tumble Book Library (subscription required)

http://www.tumblebooks.com

> Another online database of children's books, Tumble Book has a wide array of titles available. Students can have them read to them as well as read them on their own online.

World Book Online (subscription required)

http://www.worldbookonline.org

> World Book Online is a complete online encyclopedia. There are three different search interfaces depending on the level/age of the student. Includes multimedia components with many of the articles.

Figure 6.2 (*Continued*)

PebbleGo (http://www.pebblego.com) is a perfect example of a database designed for primary students. It is a great source for research but also perfect for teachers to use as literacy stations in the classroom.

Databases for young learners are very graphical in nature to make it easier for them to use in finding the information they need. The systems take advantage of audio and visual technologies to engage young learners (Young 91). As students learn about evaluating reliable sources for information, beginning them early with databases can start them off on a habit that will be useful throughout their education careers.

Many states offer statewide access to databases. Not all of the databases will be useful with elementary students, but take the time to know what is available and decide which ones fit the curriculum in the building. Alice Yucht has compiled a list of various resources by state. It is posted on her wiki (http://aliceyucht.pbworks.com/StateDatabases). Statewide access saves school districts money, as typically the state legislator, state library, or a consortium group provides the funding for them.

Databases are useful to expand the resources available in the library media center. Often students need the same volume of an encyclopedia or all want to use the same book. Databases can also help fill in gaps in the print collection as well as work as a tool to help provide resources at a variety of levels. Higher ability students who may not find the details they need in the elementary library can use the databases to locate additional information.

Make sure to send home copies of logins and passwords for home access. Parents will appreciate being able to use the resources when they are helping their students with projects or assignments at home.

Web 2.0 Applications

Web 2.0 has brought in a whole new realm of tools to use with students. Many of them are free. This is a double-edged sword because while they are free and easy to access, they were not necessarily designed for students—especially elementary students. Sites like Wordle (http://www.wordle.net), where people can create a graphical summary of text, for example, see Figure 6.3 for an example of a Wordle summarizing the text in this chapter. The more often a word is found in the text, the bigger it gets. The folks at Wordle are quick to warn their may be inappropriate language on the site since anyone can create a Wordle. They do not have the manpower to police what people post. Many of the Web 2.0 sites also keep their products free because they use advertisements. Some of these ads may not be appropriate for elementary age students, either.

This does not mean that educators should not be using these new tools. It does mean that educators need to think about how they present and use these tools with students. Educators will need to consider how to discuss the advertisement on the Web page or what to do in an instance where a student stumbles across an inappropriate word. The Internet is going to continue to be a vast resource for schools. Students are going to be using these resources with or without educators, so it becomes important to teach students how to appropriately use these resources.

As with any technology resources, the library media specialist needs to make sure to follow the district's acceptable use policy (AUP). Review it to make sure that the resources students

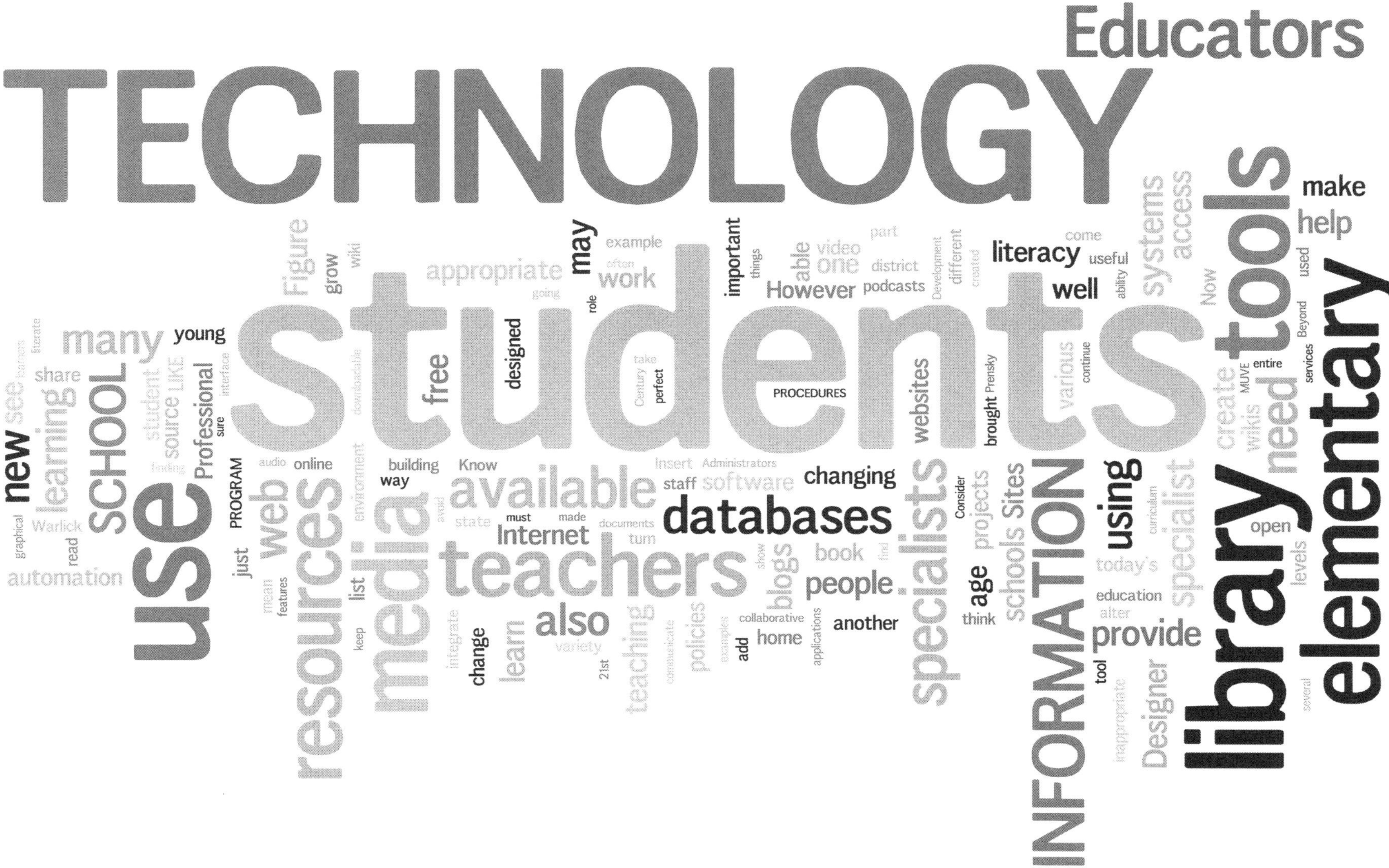

Figure 6.3   Wordle of text from Chapter 6.

are using are going to comply. Make sure to have conversations with the building administrator as projects begin to enter this environment. Administrators don't like to be caught off guard if they get a phone call from a parent asking about something their students are doing.

Many of these online tools are also blocked by Internet filters. The library media specialist should be aware of what process (if any) exists to request Web sites to be unblocked. Who makes that decision? What kind of information do they need? How much advanced time is needed to get a site unblocked? Using Web 2.0 tools require a lot of advanced planning to ensure that the experience is a successful one for students.

Each day there are new applications being launched. Keeping current requires hearing what others are trying and learning from their successes and failures. Library media specialists can use many of the resources already discussed such as listservs (e.g., LM_Net), ning (e.g., Teacher-Librarian Ning), blogs (e.g., Joyce Valenza's NeverEnding Search), Twitter (e.g., Kevin Jarrett), and so froth. The following are some of the most common applications from Web 2.0.

Wikis

Wiki is a Hawaiian word that means quick. Wikis are Web sites created quickly that any user can alter, change, add to, or subtract from. They don't require knowing HTML and are editable right from the Web. There are no files to upload to a server. They are perfect for collaborative work. Wikis track users as they make changes, so it is easy to see who is changing what and when.

There are several different Web services out on the Internet that will provide free wikis to educators. PBwork (http://www.pbworks.com) and Wikispaces (http://www.wikispaces.com) both provide ad-free wikis for educators. There are also open source options for wiki software. Consult district techs and administrators on what the best options are for using wikis with students. Examples of elementary library wikis can be found in Appendix C.

Podcasts and Vodcasts

A podcast is an audio program that is in digital format and downloadable from the Internet. It is typically updated periodically. A vodcast is a video program that is in digital format and downloadable from the Internet. The term became popular as iPods came long. The audio could be downloaded from the Web and played on an iPod or another mp3 player. For those without a device to download them to, they can still listen to them over the Internet. Some devices now also have the ability to play video as well.

Podcasts have RSS feeds (see "RSS" section later in this chapter for more information) so that people can get regular updates in their iTunes accounts ready to be downloaded into their iPods. Audacity (http://audacity.sourceforge.net/) is a free downloadable program that can be used to create podcasts. Examples of elementary library podcasts can be found in Appendix C.

Blogs

The term *blog* is short for weblog. Blogs are an online diary or journal where people can share about their lives, their hobbies, or their professions. Blogs are interactive because people can comment and carry on conversations via posts made to the blog. There are several free sites where blogs can be created. Services that provide blogs for educators to use with students include Edublogs (http://edublogs.org), Class Blogmeister (http://classblogmeister.com), and IMBEE (http://www.imbee.com/teacher). There are other sites where blogs can be created for free, but make sure to check them carefully to make sure they are appropriate for elementary students.

Another option is for the district to install blogging software on a server for student use. Wordpress is an example of open source software that is easy to use. Examples of elementary library blogs can be found in Appendix C.

Video

The most popular video source on the Internet is YouTube (http://www.youtube.com). Of course, quite likely not everything posted in YouTube adheres to the copyright laws of the United States, but there is certainly a wealth of video content available. It is important as one considers using content found on YouTube that one verifies that the content does comply with any copyright issues.

In most schools across the country, YouTube is blocked, making it difficult to use any videos found there with students. However, there are other sites that districts might consider unblocking. TeacherTube and SchoolTube are both online video sites. Both contain actual student projects, and TeacherTube has some of the best resources from YouTube available. Again, it is important to make sure that any resources found on these Web sites follow copyright guidelines before sharing them with students.

Beyond these free Web sites, Discovery Streaming and Safari Montage are subscription-based video streaming sites. They have access to a wide variety of education videos that can be downloaded.

MUVE

MUVE stands for multiuser virtual environments. The most common of those in existence is Second Life, which is for those 18 years or older. However, educators have been using Second Life for professional development with events on both the International Society for Technology in Education and American Library Association (ALA) Islands. Islands are the spaces where the avatars (users) hang out and interact with each other.

Second Life Teen is also available for students ages 13–17. These MUVE sites are mentioned merely because they are the most well known. Second Life is a growing area for professional development, but neither it nor Second Life Teen are appropriate for the elementary age audience.

There are, however, some other MUVE sites that are appropriate for elementary age students. Quest Atlantis (http://atlantis.crlt.indiana.edu) is a 3D environment for students ages 9–14. There are specific missions and quests that target a variety of academic standards. Whyville (http://www.whyville.net) is another virtual world where students can learn and interact. Whyville encourages teachers to register and bring in their entire class. As most technologies tend to trickle down, more examples of sites like these are likely to find their way into elementary schools in the years to come.

RSS

RSS stands for really simple syndication. Many Web sites, blogs, wikis, podcasts, and so forth have an RSS feed. Users can subscribe to the feed via a RSS feed reader. These readers are one place where the user can go and check to see if any of the sites he or she finds useful have been updated with new materials.

The most common RSS readers are Google Reader (http://reader.google.com) and Bloglines (http://www.bloglines.com). As a professional, the library media specialists might subscribe to the feed of bloggers who talk about library media–related issues. See Appendix B for a list of suggested blogs to follow. Instead of going to each individual site, library media specialists can go to their reader to see if any of the blogs they follow have been updated.

In an elementary school setting, the teacher might set up an account for the class and subscribe to blogs, wikis, podcasts, and so forth that connect with their current topic of studies. The resources would be helpful to both students and the teacher. Older elementary students could begin setting up their own RSS reader. Again, be sure to check the district policies before starting.

Another option is to set up a site using PageFlake (http://www.pageflakes.com) for students to view RSS feeds from. This eliminates the need for them to create an account with Google or Bloglines. The PageFlake screen might be a great activity for students to read text as part of their literacy stations.

Other Tools

An entire book could be written about Web 2.0 tools. Figure 6.4 is a sampling of just some of the available tools that might be beneficial to use with elementary age students. Remember that these tools initially were not designed for educational purposes, so be prepared that there may be some things on the various sites that are not appropriate for young children. Professional judgment and school district policies will help dictate which to try using with elementary students.

Common Craft (http://www.commoncraft.com/show) has created some very informative but simple videos that explain many of these tools and more. Check out their Web site to view the videos. They may be good examples to use with faculty and students as an introduction to using these tools.

Best Web Sites

Besides these new collaborative tools, Web sites continue to be a source of information for students and staff. Searching for resources that are accurate as well as readable by elementary age students can be challenging. See Figure 6.5 for some good places to start when looking

Below are some other Web 2.0 tools that could have potential for use with elementary students. Keep in mind that many were not designed for educational purposes, so it is possible there might be items seen on their sites that are not appropriate for elementary students.

Audacity—Software for creating podcasts and other sound recordings.
http://audacity.sourceforge.net

Bubbl—Used to create concept maps.
http://www.bubbl.us

Flickr—There are several good images here with creative commons licenses and from sources such as the Library of Congress.
http://www.flickr.com

Glogster (Education Version)—Glogs are a combination of images, photos, and sounds.
http://www.glogster.com/edu

Library Thing—Organize books in a classroom or use it to track a class reading log.
http://www.librarything.com

School Tube—Similar to YouTube, but monitored for appropriateness for students.
http://www.schooltube.com

Slide Share—An easy way to share a PowerPoint presentation.
http://www.slideshare.net

VoiceThread—Add audio to images to bring them to life.
http://voicethread.com

Wikispaces—Free wikis for educators.
http://www.wikispaces.com

Wordle—Online word cloud generator.
http://www.wordle.net

More tools are being created every day. Check out Go2Web2.0, a directory listening of tons of tools now available online.
http://www.go2web20.net

Figure 6.4   Web 2.0 tools.

Below are just a few Web sites to get one started in locating age-appropriate material for elementary students.

Dewey Browse: http://www.deweybrowse.org

Enchanted Learning: http://www.enchantedlearning.com

Eduscapes: http://www.eduscapes.com

Federal Resources for Educational Excellence: http://www.free.ed.gov

Kathy Schrock's Guide for Educators: http://school.discovery.com/schrockguide/

Pics4Learning: http://www.pics4learning.com

Read Write Think: http://www.readwritethink.org

TeachingBooks.net: http://www.teachingbooks.net paid subscription required

Thinkfinity: http://www.thinkfinity.org

Figure 6.5   Starting places for Web resources.

for new resources to use with elementary students. Some automation systems also have created services where Web sites that they have been vetted are available in the library computer catalog. Students and staff can easily access those Web sites from the catalog and avoid doing online searches with young students.

When looking for Web sites for elementary students, here are some things to consider:

- ✦ Accuracy—Is the information on the Web site correct? Is this a reliable source?
- ✦ Content—Does this provide students with the information they need? Will this help them understand the concept better?
- ✦ Reading levels—Is this Web site one students can read independently? Will they need assistance? Would it work better using it as a whole class?
- ✦ Layout—Is it easy to navigate and use the Web site?

Also consider that creating a wiki would be a quick, easy Web site where links could be posted to Web sites students need to use. Joyce Valenza has made lots of comments on her blog and in her articles that wikis make the perfect pathfinders for students. Check out her thoughts (http://informationfluency.wikispaces.com/Ten+reasons+why+your+next+pathfinder+should+be+a+wiki). The links and resources are right there to help guide students on their information-seeking journeys.

Technology Policies and Procedures

Technology polices are usually adopted by the school board based on recommendations from the superintendent and/or director of technology. The overarching document is the AUP that students and staff sign. These documents provide guidance on what is and is not permitted in the district. Beyond that, there could be a variety of other documents that provide procedures or policies dictating how staff and students will use technology.

First and foremost it is important the library media specialist be well versed in all these documents. Knowledge will help when collaborating with teachers and deciding on potential projects and technology tools to use with those projects. In addition, make sure to know the process and procedures to asking for changes to the policies. Technology continues to grow and change rapidly. Policies written just a year ago could now be out of date and stifle student learning. Library media specialists who hit roadblocks will want to draft a document that demonstrates why the policy should be changed and how it affects students and student learning. The administration might not agree to alter the policies. However, it could avoid creating a situation where there is animosity between the technology department and the library media specialist or administration and the library media specialist.

Filters

As part of national legislation, schools have installed filters on all computers in the building. The filters are designed to protect students from the inappropriate content that is out on the Web. Unfortunately, they are not 100 percent foolproof, and often in attempting to block inappropriate content, valuable and useful resources and information are also blocked.

This is the opportunity for the library media specialist to be seen as a leader in the building. How can the library media specialist build a bridge between the content students and teachers need from the Internet that is blocked and the technology department's requirement to filter the Internet? There needs to be a clearly defined process and timeline for asking for Web sites to be unblocked. The library media specialist could be part of opening the door to creating that process.

Another opportunity is to investigate options that might be easier for all involved. For example, one district has filter software installed, but all staff have a login/password to override the filter for work-related searches. While it is tracked every time they override the filter, it does give staff the ability to check out a Web site before asking for it to be unblocked.

Copyright/Creative Commons

The technology chapter is also a good place to talk about copyright. The ease of use of these tools also has made it easier for students to take pictures, text, audio, and so forth from the Internet and include them in their own projects. As library media specialists, our job continues to be to help guide students through the process. We need to help them find out how to attribute their resources or whom they need to contact to garner permission for using them.

The Web 2.0 movement has also brought along the ability for the creator to be more flexible with the licensing of their work. Creative Commons licensing allow the original creator to give the options for others to use their work, create derivatives of their work, and so forth. There are several different options. (Check out http://creativecommons.org/about/licenses/ for a complete list of the licenses.)

Just as many add the copyright symbol © to their work, they can also opt to add the symbols from the Creative Commons license. Students will want to be aware of this for two reasons: (1) They also have the option of what people can do with the work they create and (2) there are options, like through the photo Web site Flickr (http://www.flickr.com), that one can search their database by license to find images to use in presentations.

Wiki Wrap-Up

The amazing speed of technology has ushered the world into the 21st century. For students, this is all they've known. For teachers, this may be a foreign environment. For library media specialists, this is an opportunity to help bridge the gap from student to teacher. Library media specialists can help guide teachers through these technologies and the process of changing their instruction to meet the demands of the students of the 21st century. For additional resources, check out the companion wiki Web site (http://www.carl-harvey.com/librarytieswiki/).

Works Cited

Prensky, Marc. "Digital Natives, Digital Immigrants." *On the Horizon* 9, no. 5 (October 2001). http://www.marcprensky.com/writing/Prensky%20-%20Digital%20Natives,%20Digital%20Immigrants%20-%20Part1.pdf.

Warlick, David F. *Redefining Literacy 2.0* (2nd ed.). Columbus, OH: Linworth Publishing, 2009.

Young, Terrence E., Jr. "It's Elementary." *School Library Journal* 50 (June 2004): 91.

Zmuda, Allison, and Violet H. Harada. *Librarians as Learning Specialists: Meeting the Learning Imperative for the 21st Century.* Westport, CT: Libraries Unlimited, 2008.

CHAPTER 7

Library Administration

Develop a system that works for you. It doesn't have to conform to anyone else's standards, as long as it's something that you can function within.

—J'aimé L. Foust, *Dewey Need to Get Organized?*

While the majority of the library media specialist's time should be devoted to working with students and staff, time must still be devoted to the administrative tasks of operating a library media center. The job can be made easier by setting up policies and procedures, planning ahead, and using technology tools to help keep the library running smoothly and efficiently.

Policies and Procedures

Policies are the guiding documents from the school board or administrators on how the library media center should be run. Policies might include a technology policy, selection policy, challenged materials policy, collection development policy, or even a policy regarding the type of schedule a library operates. Library media specialists often provide input or suggestions as policies are created, while the final decision typically rests with an administrator or the school board.

Procedures are step-by-step instructions on how to complete a specific task. Procedures could be for students, teachers, library staff, or the library media specialist. Procedures provide a blueprint so that there is no confusion about how to complete a certain task. Procedures are typically developed by the library media specialist and do not require approval by the school board. Make sure to share them with the principal just so he or she can be on the same wavelength. The administrator will let the library media specialist know if he has concerns. It is also a good idea to include the stakeholders in helping to develop procedures, too. If the library media specialist is working on student procedures, let students chime in with ideas and suggestions.

It may be difficult to write procedures with every class in the school. The library media center needs to have consistent procedures for all grades, so consider using the student library advisory group to write the procedures. When students are part of the development process, they have more ownership of the procedures. The process is the same for procedures for other groups. For example, consider asking the library advisory committee to help write any procedures for the staff.

When policies and procedures are clearly written out and shared with stakeholders, there is common understanding of how the library media center is to run. It eliminates confusion and allows the program to run smoothly. Some possible areas or ideas for procedures could include: circulation, ordering, processing materials, daily to-do items, weekly to-do items, monthly to-do items, beginning of the year checklist, end of the year checklist, student behavior and expectations, recess procedures, and so forth. Policies and procedures are necessary to ensure that everyone can take full advantage of everything the library media center has to offer.

Library Media Center Policies

Policies might (or should) include a selection of instructional materials, a challenge policy, and an acceptable use policy for technology. If these policies don't exist, begin the conversation to begin developing them. Follow the proper chain of command in talking with the building administrator and central office administrators who might coordinate the library media program, and then the superintendent. Make sure to have examples and data to support the needed policies.

The California Department of Education provides some links to sample policies on their Web site at (http://www.cde.ca.gov/ci/cr/lb/policies.asp). Some districts set very specific policies such as check-out limits or flexible versus fixed schedules for the entire district, whereas other districts will allow the individual buildings to make those decisions.

Library media specialists in the 21st century will want to keep up with how the landscape is changing in their media centers. What policies will need to be created to deal with new formats and resources in the collection? What policies will need to be created (or modified) to bring in the new technology tools available to students and staff?

Library Media Center Procedures

Student Procedures

Student procedures could include things like: how to check out a book, how to use a shelf marker, or how to select a book (see Figure 7.1 for sample procedures). Procedures should be positive but detailed. These procedures give students clear expectations for completing a task. When there are problems or behavior issues, referring to the procedures while discussing the issue with students provides a very clear picture of what the students were supposed to be doing. Creating common procedures throughout the building also creates a consistent environment for students. They know the expectation no matter where in the school they go.

CHIME PROCEDURES

When you hear the chimes, use **COOPERATION** to stop what you are doing and listen for directions.

STORY STEPS PROCEDURES

Use **EFFORT** to come into the Story Steps quietly.

Use **COMMON SENSE** to walk up and down the Story Steps.

Use **RESPONSIBILITY** to keep your hands and feet to yourself.

Use **INTEGRITY** to be an active listener.

IPOD PROCEDURES

Use **RESPECT** to ask a teacher to check out the iPod. Teachers and students will need to use **ORGANIZATION** to keep track of the iPod in the classroom.

Use **FLEXIBILITY** to only keep the iPod for one week, so that others may enjoy using them.

Teachers will use **CURIOSITY** to consider using the iPods as a Literacy Station.

Use **EFFORT** to make sure to handle the iPod with care.

Use **COOPERATION** to share the iPod with other students in the classroom.

RECESS PROCEDURES

✦ Students are welcome to come to the library media center during recess.
✦ Students will:

—use **RESPECT** to not disturb classes who are using the library media center.

—use **RESPONSIBILITY** to ask for permission to leave the library during recess.

—use **CURIOSITY** to quietly play with the puppets, read a book, read a magazine, explore the math or writing center, and/or find a quiet place to spend recess.

—use **COMMON SENSE** when playing with the puppets to choose one puppet at a time and returning puppets back to the puppet stands.

—use **INTEGRITY** to watch the clock and return back to class when recess is over.

BOOK CHECK-OUT PROCEDURES

Use **COMMON SENSE** to check out the number of items for which you can be responsible.

Fiction books check out for two weeks; all other items check out for one week.

You may renew an item one time unless another student is waiting for the item.

Use **RESPONSIBILITY** to return your books on time. Overdue items must be returned to check out new items.

Use **PATIENCE** to ask to put a book on reserve if it is currently checked out.

Use **RESPONSIBILITY** to find a nice and safe place to keep library materials while they are at home. If materials are lost or damaged, students will have to pay the replacement cost.

Figure 7.1 Sample student procedures.

Procedures drastically cut down on discipline issues. Not following procedures should have a natural consequence. It could be the elimination of something fun to give time to practice the procedures that were not being followed.

Consider taking video of students who are following correct procedures. Use these on the morning announcements or as part of a lesson to review the procedure with other students. Post them on the school Web site so that parents can see the expectation of students doing the right thing. Consider a procedure wall of fame. Students who are caught following the procedures get their picture added to the wall of fame.

Procedures should be posted. Tape checkout procedures to the checkout desk. Hang up procedures for the story steps area of the library in the story steps area. In elementary schools, this not only reinforces the procedures but also is another place where students will find text to read. Procedures can also be posted online, kept in binders, or written on a poster to hang on the wall. Whatever the format, the important thing is that they are easily accessible.

Staff Procedures

Procedures for staff are also a smart idea. Such procedures create a common understanding and can help foster a collegial working environment. Some examples might include procedures for signing up or scheduling time to work with the library media specialist, bringing their classes to the library media center, textbook distribution, accessing technology resources, or laminating resources. See Figure 7.2 for sample staff procedures.

Library Media Staff Procedures

Procedures for library support staff are going to cover many of the day-to-day operations. They could also include procedures for volunteers, student helpers, and so forth. Procedures also help library support staff because they relieve the burden of being the decision maker when working with students and teachers. Staff are merely following the procedures that were already outlined. Procedures give them clear guidance when a decision needs to be made. Procedures should be written down and kept together for easy access. Procedures in turn also become a training manual when staff or volunteers move on. See Figure 7.3 for sample staff procedures.

Library Media Specialist Procedures

It is also a good idea to create procedures for the library media specialist. What tasks does the library media specialist do on a regular basis? What tasks does the library media specialist need to be reminded to do? Procedures help to provide structure and organization, so it is another way to help the library media specialist stay organized. See Figure 7.4 for library media specialist procedures. The procedures also are helpful to the library media specialists that follow at that school. They can give them guidance on how things worked and give them a basis for taking the existing program and making it even better.

POSTER MAKER MACHINE PROCEDURES	LAMINATING PROCEDURES
✦ Posters made on the poster maker cost the school approximately $4.00 per poster. Please make sure the settings are correct before you start printing. We don't want to waste paper by having to reprint mistakes. ✦ Place items face down. ✦ Press Start/Clear. Please see a library assistant if you need assistance.	✦ Please make sure to choose items that will have lasting value to laminate. ✦ Items will be laminated on Monday and Wednesday. ✦ Items dropped off by 10 A.M., should be ready by the end of the day. ✦ Items will be put in the teacher's mailboxes for pick-up.

WHO DO I ASK?	
Library Media Specialist	Collaboration for instruction, instructional materials (print, nonprint, and computer), leveled library, interlibrary loan requests, reading incentive program, library media center Web page resources, and professional development.
Tech or Media Assistant	Problems with voice mail, e-mail, computer networking, computers problems, printer problems, printer cartridges, simple software assistance questions, and overhead bulbs.
Tech or Media Assistant	Circulation problems, lost books, and overdue books.
Library Media Specialist	Technology hardware, software, and A/V needs (ordering additional copies of software, replacing old equipment, etc.) The library media specialist will work with the principal to determine purchasing decisions.
Library Media Specialist	Anything else? We're sure there are things we've missed. So, if there is, let me know and we'll figure out who can best help.

Figure 7.2 Sample staff procedures.

OPENING PROCEDURES	WEEKLY PROCEDURES
Turn on all computers.	Water the plants.
Unlock and open all doors.	Back up the automation system.
Check voicemail and e-mail.	Run overdue notices.
Log in to/set up automation system.	Run reserve pick-up notices.
Check in any materials in the book drop.	Check to see what needs to be done to keep the library neat and organized.
Check calendar for today's schedule and special events.	
Freshen up any displays with new titles.	
Check "To Do List" dry erase board.	

Figure 7.3 Sample library media center staff procedures.

ORDERING PROCEDURES

Choose materials to order.

Determine if funds are available in accounts.

Give to assistant to enter in the accounting system.

Electronically sign to OK the purchase (principal and central office will also sign off electronically).

Blue copy of the purchase order sent to library media specialist.

When all items are arrived, sign off on blue copy and send to central office. Include any bills that are also received as well.

WEEKLY PROCEDURES

Send out weekly Web site.

Update collaboration log.

Attend weekly planning sessions.

MONTHLY PROCEDURES

Send monthly report to principal

Review previous year's collaboration log to preview what might be ahead and to spark conversations with teachers.

Update library media center Web site.

Figure 7.4 Sample library media specialist procedures.

The Learning Space

Procedures can also be needed because of the physical learning environment of the library media center. Thinking of the needs of the elementary library media center facilities in the coming years leads one to ask questions like:

✦ What kind of space will be needed to house materials?

✦ What kind of space will be needed for whole-class instruction?

✦ What kind of space will be needed for students to work in small groups?

✦ What kind of space will be needed for students to use technology to produce audio, video, and so forth?

✦ What kind of technology resources will students need in the library media center?

Housing materials has always been a primary role of the library media center. Likely there are few libraries that have space or storage that is underutilized. For the elementary library, shelving will still be key because the printed book is a valuable tool for teaching students how to read. While electronic formats and options continue to become available, there is still demand for the printed book.

In addition to shelving for books, there will need to be options for materials in a variety of formats such as audiobooks, Playaways, CDs, DVDs, equipment, and other formats that we may not even know about yet.

Teaching and learning is one of the primary roles of the library media specialist. Having sufficient space to work is important. Are there multiple areas in the library media center where classes could be working such as a tables/chairs area or a story step area? Beyond the space in the library media center, remember that the walls have come tumbling down in the 21st century. If there isn't sufficient space, is it possible to work in the classroom. Where can the students be the most successful? David V. Loertscher, Carol Joechlin, and Sandi Zwaan in their book *The New Learning Commons: Where Learners Win* refer to the library media centers where students come and go to get the support they need. It is the center of learning of the school. It's a place to find best practices. It's a place for students to share what they have learned.

As part of that learning commons, there need to also be areas where students can work independently or in small groups. Are there places where they cluster together on a project? Are there comfortable seating areas? Can students utilize space on the floor to work? Unless a new facility is being built, many library media specialists inherit the space they have. Thinking outside the box a bit can get the creative juices flowing to think of alternative ideas when the walls can't be torn down.

Producing information with technology will require access to these tools as well. Is there a quiet place where a filming studio could be set up for those who want to make video or audio projects? Are their simple to use cameras such as FlipVideo cameras or digital cameras available for students to use? How about computer access? Is the library media center wireless? Are there laptops available that students can use? Are there desktop machines that students can use? Determining what resources are available will help dictate how to lay out the space.

Steven Baule in his book *Facilities Planning for School Library and Technology Centers* offers a checklist for library media specialists and designing teams to consider when planning a new facility. He divides the checklist up into program questions, student control and access, instruction, furniture, library workroom and office, circulation/service desk, audio/visual equipment, noise levels, flooring, Americans with Disabilities Act requirements, display areas, and other. While many of the questions will only apply to places that are in the design phase, consider reviewing the checklist with an already built facility. Knowing the limitations of the space, what changes can be made to make the library media center ready for the 21st-century learner?

Appealing Environment

Library media centers should be inviting places. Students should want to come there. Not only is the library media center a place for information resources, but it is also a place that students can find opportunities to play, to explore, and to learn from books, magazines, and games. Students should feel free to ask questions and seek help. They should want to come and use the facility as a place to work as well. The library media center has the potential to have a variety of uses, but it is just an empty space without the students!

Whether the library media center is a brand new facility or one built decades ago, the library media specialist has to work to make the place warm and inviting. Use the tops of the shelves not only as a place to display books but also as a place to add photos of students working in the library or pictures of their favorite authors. Include plants and stuffed animals to bring the tops of the shelves to life. Strategically place items where they can be helpful to students locating information (e.g., a stuffed animal of a dog or cat near the pet books).

Materials should be easy for students to access. If the shelves are too tall, remove materials from the top shelves and turn them into display areas. Highlight student work in the shelves that are too high for materials. Hang up work from art classes, or display other types of projects students have done.

Another important activity is to get rid of the junk. If the library media center is cluttered, full of old and outdated stuff, it begins to look just like the old stuff it is housing. Keeping things for "some day" is not always wise—especially in small places. Weeding the collection is important. Books that are falling apart or have dated covers are not going to appeal to 21st-century students. New books can get lost behind all the old junk. Do not limit the purging to just the materials. Furniture can pile up. Each piece of furniture in the library media center should have a current and relevant purpose. If it doesn't, it needs to go. Space is too important to keep something that no one is using. Opening up the library by eliminating the old and dated materials and furniture can free up space and make it more inviting to students.

Sometimes, however, old furniture is all there is. How can it be dressed up to make it more appealing? Can it be covered with fabric? Could it be painted? While it might not be exactly what is needed, it may be that by trying to dress the furniture up can be made workable. Make sure to check with maintenance staff or the building administrator so that whatever changes you make are still compatible with fire codes or district standards. Another option is to see what might be in the school storage. Sometimes there are things being stored that might work better than the stuff already in the library media center.

Besides furniture, display materials are also an important part of the environment. Are there places to display new books or books on a specific theme? Look at examples in the public library, bookstore, or other school libraries. How do they draw the reader in to find fabulous books? For example, one school used an old computer table, covered it with fabric, put a wire display wrack on it and labeled it "Our Favorites." Then near the display, they put blank bookmarks that say, "This is one of [insert name of teacher or student]'s favorite books. When you finish reading it, let him/her know what you think." Teachers or students can add their favorite books to the display and write their names on the bookmark. Other students can come along and choose books recommended by their teacher or fellow classmates. The display is mall, re-uses old furniture, and serves a purpose to promote books to students!

Wall space is always another way to add character and appeal to the library media center. It is possible to go overboard. Just because there is empty wall space does not mean it needs to be filled. Wall space can serve to promote the library as well as instructional resources. Promotional things could include hanging up a display to focus on a specific author or theme. Maybe there is a monthly calendar of author birthdays. Use bulletin board space to promote library programs or special projects happening in the library media center.

The other option for wall space is for instructional resources. Near the computer it would make sense to hang up information about online databases, tips for using the library computer catalog, and how to save student work. Many schools use a word wall in their classrooms where they put up in alphabetical order key words they want students to learn. If teachers in the school have one, so should the library media center. However, the focus should be on vocabulary that is specific to working in the library media center. Another option instead of a word wall is to match those words with pictures and then display them in a more random, visually appealing way. This helps students connect the picture to the text and still provides a way to stress and teach library-related vocabulary.

Wall space also should be reserved to hang up procedures. Students need to know what is expected, so procedures should be posted for students to easily see when they need a reminder. Remember, however, that when posters are covering every square inch of free space it makes the library feel closed in and cluttered. Strategically pick and choose those things that will be the most helpful to students.

Schedules

Fixed or flexible schedule? The debate about the best type of schedule for a library media center has never really been settled. It likely will continue to be debated well into the next century. Most would agree that flexible is the ideal, but the reality in many elementary schools across the country is that the library media program is on a fixed schedule. In the November 2001 *School Library Journal,* Doug Johnson wrote one of the most infamous articles in the flexible versus fixed debate ("It's Good to Be Inflexible," http://www.doug-johnson.com/dougwri/real-flexibility.html), in which he gave his rationale for fixed schedules. On his Web site, readers can also see the pro and con responses he received.

Fixed schedules give every student a regularly scheduled opportunity to be in the library media center. The library media specialist provides preparation time for teachers, so the teacher usually does not remain with the students. Library media specialists are responsible for instruction and also for the time that students check out materials. See Figure 7.5 for the positives and negatives of a fixed schedule.

POSITIVES	NEGATIVES
✦ Every student guaranteed time in the library media center each week.	✦ There is often no communication between the library media specialist and classroom teacher.
✦ There is no reliance on the teacher and library media specialist communicating.	✦ Learning in the library media center often does not connect to what is happening in the classroom.
✦ Teachers have release time for preparation.	✦ Skills are taught in isolation without meaning to students.
	✦ Projects take extended times because students may only get to the library once a week.

Figure 7.5   Positives/negatives of fixed schedules.

Flexible scheduling of the library media center provides no formal schedule. Students come to check out materials whenever they want. Instruction relies on the library media specialist collaborating with the classroom teacher. Students from a particular class or grade level may come down for several days in a row to work on a unit, and then it may be a few weeks before they are back for the next project. This flexibility allows the library media specialist to work in-depth with students rather than just once every few days for a set amount of time. See Figure 7.6 for the positives and negatives of a flexible schedule.

Either schedule relies heavily on the building administrator and on the library media specialist. The administrator has the control over how the schedule is organized in the building unless the schedule is based on a contract with the teachers' union. If it is not a state or district mandate, the administrator can determine if the library will operate on a fixed of flexible schedule. The administrator can also be a driving factor when a flexible schedule is implemented. If the administrator expects teachers to work with the library media specialist, then she can make sure that all students have the instruction and opportunities in the library media center. The same kind of impact can be felt based on the role that the library media specialist takes. On a fixed schedule, while it can be more difficult because of time constraints, the library media specialist can still work to collaborate with teachers and connect instruction in the library media center to what is being taught in the classroom. On the flexible schedule side, the library media specialist needs to be the proactive element that goes out to work with teachers. She needs to be touting the skills students need to learn and suggesting opportunities where the classroom teacher and library media specialist can work together to design instruction.

Peggy Milam Creighton, in her November 2007 article in *Library Media Connection* titled "Just How Flexible Are We?," updates the status of implementing flexible scheduling. She summarizes the current research that says that more than half of the elementary schools in the country are on a fixed schedule and that the majority are either fixed or a combination despite the research that says flexible schedules are more beneficial for student achievement.

Looking at 21st-century students and the skills they will need, it becomes harder and harder to squeeze those skills into 40-minute lessons every few days. Students (and teachers) will need to devote more time for students to work on projects. They'll need support from the library media specialist at different points along the way. The fixed schedule will make it difficult for students to get access to the library media center and library media specialist at the point of need.

Beyond just instruction and circulation, the facility itself also becomes very limited on a fixed schedule. Many media centers not only have an instructional area of tables/chairs, but also a story step area, as well as an area with all the shelving. Sometimes these are separate areas and sometimes they are intertwined. When the areas are separated, the facility can be utilized by more than one class. A flexible schedule library media center could accommodate many classes at the same time all doing different things. For example, class A could be at the table/chairs area working on a research project, class B could be in the story area performing a readers' theatre or listening to a guest speaker, classes C and D could be checking out books, and class E might also be doing research in a computer lab adjacent to the library media center. This does not include individual students who might be using the library media center for a variety of activities including research, recreational reading, and so forth. The largest classroom in the schools becomes better utilized when a flexible schedule is implemented. See Figure 7.7 for a sample facility schedule form.

POSITIVES	NEGATIVES
✦ Requires library media specialist and classroom teacher to communicate. ✦ Students may come multiple times to the library media center for circulation and instruction. ✦ Projects are completed in a timely fashion because students can come for multiple days in a row. ✦ Learning in the library is connected to learning in the classroom. ✦ Library media specialist can attend planning sessions held during teacher prep time.	✦ Some teachers may opt to not come for instruction or circulation leaving some students with gaps in their skills.

Figure 7.6 Positives/negatives of flexible schedules.

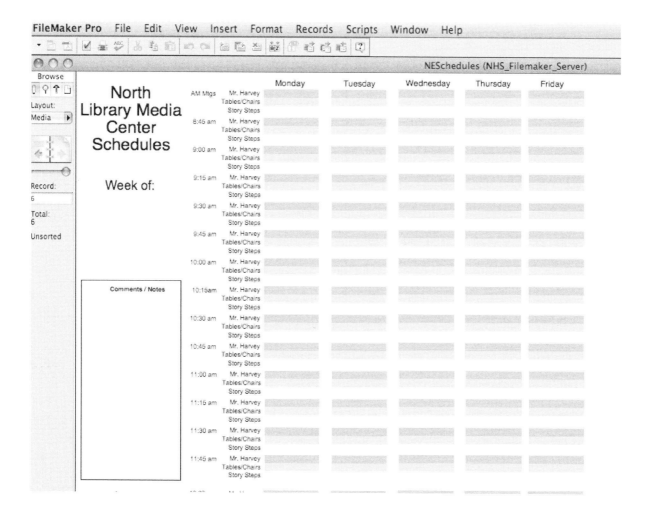

This is a sample schedule for the Library Media Center at North Elementary School

The first line is for the library media specialist.
The next line is for the tables/chairs area.
The last line is for the story step area.

Teachers can sign up for the areas but are only able to view the library media specialist schedule. To sign up with the library media specialist, they must have a collaborative planning conversation.

Figure 7.7   Sample facilities schedule for flexible scheduled library.

There is little doubt that this debate will rage on for years to come. There is no magic wand that will be waived to solve the problem. *Empowering Learners: Guidelines for School library Media Programs,* published by American Association of School Librarians (AASL) in 2009, lists flexible scheduling as the ideal for all school library media centers. We know that often the schedule is out of the hands of the library media specialist. However, it is important to be aware of the best practices, aware of the needs of the students, and be able to articulate this information to those who can make those decisions because that's what children of the 21st century are going to need.

Long-Range Planning

Long-range planning is important for two reasons: (A) It forces an assessment of where the program is now and (B) Creates a roadmap of where the program needs to go. The long-range plan is how to get from A to B. This would be part of the role of the library media advisory committee. Having input from various stakeholders builds a stronger plan, and it creates people invested in helping the library media program get from A to B. Long-range plans can focus on the entire library media program or can be compartmentalized to special areas or parts.

The Department of Instruction in Wisconsin has posted an online page (http://dpi.wi.gov/imt/slmplngrng.html) describing long-range planning for school library media programs. Also available online is a planning guide for Massachusetts school library media centers, *School Library Media Center Long-Range Planning Guide: A Workbook for Massachusetts School Library Media Centers* (http://www.nmrls.org/youth/school.doc). Both provide instructions for what should be in the plan and how to create it.

Long-range plans should be for three to five years. Aligning the plans to the school improvement plan is critical. How can what the library media program does affect student success? The plan should address those elements. The plan will encompass the entire program—instruction, collections, budgets, technology, and so forth. All the elements overlap to create a successful program, and that starts with a successful plan.

Instruction

Creating long-term lesson plans or a curriculum map of the library media program's instruction is very helpful in planning different classes working on different skills and units. The curriculum map creates a visual to help with the collection development as discussed earlier in this chapter.

In Figure 4.15 there is a sample of a yearlong plan/curriculum map for the library media program. With this map, the library media specialist can determine what grade levels or specific teachers he needs to target. He can also look at where there may be gaps in instruction.

If there is already an instruction plan in place, with all the new resources and standards from AASL, International Society for Technology in Education (ISTE), and the Partnership for the 21st Century (P21), it is quite likely time for it to be updated. The instruction plan should be in a constant state of flex. As standards change, as the needs of students change, and as technology changes, the plan should be able to be altered and adapted.

Collections

Library media center collections are a great example of where a systematic long-range plan is helpful. Having a plan on how to keep the collection current and improve it can be instrumental in getting additional funding dollars. Library automation software collects statistics and data about the collection. Most systems will tell the average copyright dates for each section.

Use curriculum mapping to determine what areas in the collection are most critical to the curriculum taught in the school. While library media center collections strive to cover a wide range of topics like the public library, school library media specialists are much more driven by curriculum, so the collection should reflect that. Also gain input from the teachers and students. While the collection may have sufficient resources on a topic, are there a variety of reading levels available to meet all the students' needs? Are there sufficient materials to meet students' recreational reading needs? Input from others will be another data point in helping to determine the plan. Are there sufficient resources that students and teachers need based on the school improvement plan and building goals? What about student wants and interests?

An effective long-range plan addresses more than just print resources. The library media specialist needs to assess the electronic resources as well. What databases are available? What online Web sites are available (and reliable)? These should factor into decisions about what resources need to be purchased. It may make more sense to subscribe to online databases than to add additional print resources on a topic.

Technology

Technology is another area where long-range planning is a must. Attending any of the technology conferences, one can quickly see that the availability of technology focused on education is massive. There are countless gadgets, tools, software, and pieces of equipment ready for the purchasing. As with building the collection, there should be some sort of systematic approach to purchasing technology.

The degree of influence the library media specialist has on spending technology dollars varies by school district. In some districts, all those decisions are made at the district level. In other districts, those decisions are made at the building level. Regardless of the level the decisions are made at, it is a good idea to know what the plan is and, whenever possible, be part of the decision making process.

Just like the collections in the library, technology tools are important for students. Looking at the AASL, ISTE, and Partnership for the 21st Century Skills standards, one can see that there is no way to avoid students being engrossed in using these online resources. With so many choices out there, it is also important to make careful and deliberate decisions on what tools are the highest priorities. As more and more resources become available online (for free and by subscription), selection of these tools increases in importance.

Finally, predicting what technology is coming will help guide which professional development is needed in the building. As library media specialists have a key role in providing professional development, it is important that there is a plan in place for how to help teachers learn these new tools.

Work with the administrator and library media advisory committee to determine needs and desires. Share these with administrators and district technology staff to see what might be possible. The library media specialist can be the critical link between the technology department, administration, and teachers.

The library media advisory committee will think about all these areas. They may go back and survey teachers, students, parents, and so forth. They may want input from the central office about future plans for the district. They may want to review any data collected by the library media specialist (circulation, instruction, and so forth).

Once they see the data, it is time to determine the plan. Along with the library media specialist, the library media advisory committee can look at the data and help determine priorities. What area needs the most work? What areas can wait a little while? What areas are in good shape? Make a plan on what needs to be done to help strengthen those areas that are lacking. Be sure to create estimates of what funds will be needed as well.

The last step is to match funding with needs. Quite likely the funding will not be enough to cover all the things needed. The plan puts out on the radar what the library media program needs. Principals, who are part of the library advisory committee, will know, if additional funds become available, exactly how they would affect the library media program. The library media specialist knows that he or she can also begin looking out for other funding sources as well. In times of tough finances, a multiple approach to funding will be important.

Evaluating the Library Media Program

It is important to undertake the process of evaluating the library media program on a regular basis. Decisions made in today's schools are data driven. An important role for library media specialists is to collect data about their programs. They need to see what is working and what they can make even better. One of the ways to get better is to analyze the data and determine strategies to implement. Library media specialists need to know if they are providing the services, the resources, and the opportunities that students and teachers need and want.

Collecting Data

Surveys

The simplest way to find out what people think is to ask. A quick survey is easy to send out and get responses back. Traditional paper/pencil surveys can easily go into mailboxes, but consider using one of the online survey tools like SurveyMonkey, Zoomerrang, or Polldaddy. Online survey tools can instantly calculate and provide the results of the survey. See Figure 7.8 for a sample annual staff survey and Figure 7.9 for an annual student survey. By just tweaking the survey from year to year, the library media specialist can see trends and determine potential areas for improvement or change.

_____ Teacher   _____ Support Staff   _____ Other

Scale: 1–4 with 1 being the lowest and 4 being the highest. If the question does not apply to your role in the building, just leave it blank.

Instruction

	1	2	3	4
1. The library media specialist (LMS) is easily available for coplanning, coteaching, and coassessment.				
2. I have coplanned with the LMS this year.				
3. The LMS is proactive to suggest ideas for activities or lessons.				
4. I am comfortable going and asking the LMS for help.				
5. Students are free to come and use the library media center(LMC) at any time.				
6. The LMS regularly communicates with the staff about programming and resources using a variety of methods.				
7. The LMS provides help to me on an individual basis.				
8. The LMS provides staff development opportunities.				
9. The LMS is an integral part of the curriculum instruction at our school.				
10. The LMC provides support for reading motivation.				
11. The annual author visit is a good use of time and resources.				
12. The LMS supports my work in meeting school improvement goals.				
13. The LMS provides instruction that supports school improvement goals.				

14. What are (if any) stumbling blocks to using the LMS more to help with instruction of your students?

15. How could the LMS more effectively help you with instruction?

16. How could the library media program support the school improvement goals?

Facilities and Resources

	1	2	3	4
17. The LMC facility is welcoming and inviting.				
18. The LMC is always available when I need it.				
19. My students come at least once a week to check out new materials.				
20. I use the LMC catalog in my classroom.				
21. I use the LMC catalog with state standards search.				

Figure 7.8   Annual staff survey.

	1	2	3	4
22. I use video streaming resources.				
23. I use electronic databases available from the LMC.				
24. The library media center has sufficient resources to meet the curriculum.				
25. The resources that are available meet my curriculum and academic standards. They are current and up-to-date.				
26. I recommended resources in our parent library to parents.				
27. I use the leveled library resources.				

28. In what areas (if any) do you wish the LMC could provide more resources?

29. What are stumbling blocks to accessing the available online tools?

30. What additional resources do you need to meet school improvement goals?

General Information

	1	2	3	4
31. The library facility is available for my use when needed.				
32. The library support staff is efficient in responding to my needs.				
33. The library check out/in procedures are efficient and effective.				

34. What is the most useful part of the library media program?

35. What services do you wish the library media program offered that aren't currently available?

36. List the way(s) you think the library media program could be improved to better serve students and staff.

37. What areas would you like more staff development on in the areas of media/technology?

38. Other comments/concerns/or thoughts?

Figure 7.8   (*Continued*)

Elementary Student Survey

	YES	Not Sure	NO
1. Do you like coming to the library media center?	☺	😐	☹
2. When you come to the library media center, do you learn new things?	☺	😐	☹
3. When you come to the library media center can you get answers to your questions?	☺	😐	☹
4. When you come to the library media center, do you learn how to find information?	☺	😐	☹
5. Can you find books you want to read in our library media center?	☺	😐	☹
6. Can you find books to answer your questions in our library media center?	☺	😐	☹
7. Do you use the library media center Web page?	☺	😐	☹

8. What do you like best about the library media center?

9. If you could change one thing about our library media center, what would it be?

Secondary Study Survey—Answer the questions below. Please give examples to support your answer.

1. What are the things in our library media center that make you want to come here to study, learn, read, use technology, and socialize?

2. When you come to the library media center who or what helps you most as you search for answers to your questions?

3. When you come to the library media center, which types of technology and software are most helpful as you try to find information?

Figure 7.9 Annual student survey.

4. What types and subjects of books would you like to find more of in our library media center?

5. What other technologies would you find helpful as you seek answers for your questions in our library media center?

6. What are the most helpful features of the library media center Web page? Which do you use most?

7. What do you like best about the library media center?

8. If you could change one thing about our library media center, what would it be?

Figure 7.9 (*Continued*)

Anecdotal Conversations

Listen to what students, staff, administrators, and parents say about the library media program. Take all their suggestions as constructive. Consider how what they say about the program can be used to make it better. What advice warrants changes in the program? What advice is best to ignore? The library media specialist will have to filter out some mean comments because the people saying them often don't have the context for what they are saying.

Another piece of anecdotal data consists of the e-mails, notes, cards, and so forth that the library media specialist receives from students, staff, parents, and so forth. Consider creating a happy file. This is a place to file letters, notes, or cards. As e-mails have become more of a method for communication, create a file on the computer to download those e-mails that contain praise for the program and the library media specialist. These pieces of data are helpful when telling the story of the library media center. At the same time, when things are not going as well, take a few minutes to revisit the happy file. It will help rejuvenate the library media specialist to get up and begin to tackle the problems he or she may be facing at that point.

Statistics

Libraries offer many opportunities to collect statistics. How many items circulated this month? How many classes came in to the library media center this month? Statistics are important because they help tell part of the story of what is happening in the library media center.

The time and effort collecting and analyzing statistics is very important, but do not let it become overwhelmingly time consuming. Just because there are statistics that can be collected does not mean all data are worthy of collection. The library media specialist needs to determine what statistics are really going to tell a compelling and effective story about the library media program.

Consider a principal whose focus is totally on literacy. The data provided to him might show how much the students in his building are checking out materials. The per pupil checkout limit is much higher than any other school in the district. The principal is also interested in the leveled library. The library media specialist makes sure to include these two data points in every monthly report. Focus on telling the story of how the library media program is helping to support these programs.

Rationale for Data Collection

The main reason to collect data is to determine how best to help students learn. To that end, the data collected is important because it helps tell the story of the library media center and provides directions on how the program can get even better for the kids next year. Both are valid reasons for spending time analyzing data, but each might require different kinds of data to help accomplish the goal.

Keeping track of the grade levels and teachers that work with the library media specialist can be important so that the media specialist can meet with a teacher whose participation is lower than in the past. Noting a drop-off in participation, the library media specialist can go and talk with the teacher and get her collaborating once again in the library. Examining circulation statistics and seeing a drop or a gain can help determine what might need to be done in the library to bring students in to check out materials or decide what has been working well so one can continue to see the circulation grow.

Additional questions one might ask involve standardized test scores. How does what happen in the library media center affect those scores? There need to be data and evidence to prove to administrators the strong link between the test scores and the library media center.

Sharing the Results

Not only is it important to collect and analyze data to help the library media specialist make the program even better, it is also important to use that data to help tell the library media specialist's story to others. Chapter 3 provides a variety of communication methods for sharing the good news with various stakeholders. Data is an important way to help tell the story of the effective library media center.

Modesty has gone out of style. Library media specialists need to be sharing all the great things they are doing with their teachers, their administrators, their parents, and their students. All the stakeholders need to know the great things happening in that library media center so they can go out and tell others.

Library Media Specialist Evaluation

Each district has their own method for evaluating teachers. In some places, the evaluation method and tool are different for the library media specialist than for the classroom teacher, while in other places the form is exactly the same. Each system has its pluses and minuses.

South Carolina, which has a statewide evaluation structure, for example, has posted a specific tool to evaluation library media specialists (http://www.scteachers.org/adept/lms.cfm). This separate form takes into consideration that there are many elements outside the job of a classroom teacher that a library media specialist does. Many believe these should be included and recognized in the evaluation of the library media specialist.

Other districts evaluate the library media specialist on the teacher rubric. This rubric may have some items that don't apply to the library media specialist, but overall much of the focus on teaching and learning is important for both library media specialists and classroom teachers. At the same time, an astute administrator should be able to observe what a library media specialist does and assess those outside duties as they apply. Library media specialists should also be making sure their administrators are aware of the various roles and tasks they complete. Between the two of them it is possible to make the teacher rubric workable.

There are benefits to either having a unique form or using the teacher form. The unique form makes it easy to observe the other jobs performed by the library media specialist, but at the same time sets them apart from all the other teachers in the building. Using the same form as teachers makes the administrator focus on the instructional role of the library media specialist, but they may end up missing some of the behind-the-scenes jobs preformed.

Whether in a district with one form for all or a district with a special form for the library media specialist, the important element is the education of the administrator. When the administrator is filling out the evaluation, can he or she describe the library media program you have and do they know what the next steps are to take it to the next level? Whatever the tool, the library media specialist needs to keep the lines of communication open with administrators to help demonstrate to them what the library media program (and library media specialist) of the 21st century should be.

Wiki Wrap-Up

One thing that hasn't changed in the 21st century is that there are still administrative tasks that have to be done to run an effective library media center. Technology tools in the 21st century have made some of those tasks easier. Having the administrative side of the library running smoothly can allow the library media specialist to focus on the instructional role. For additional resources, check out the companion wiki Web site (http://www.carl-harvey.com/librarytieswiki/).

Works Cited

American Association of School Librarians. *Empowering Learners: Guidelines for School Library Media Programs.* Chicago: American Association of School Librarians, 2007.

Baule, Steven M. *Facilities Planning for School Library and Technology Centers* (2nd ed.). Columbus, OH: Linworth Publishing, 2007.

Creighton, Peggy Milam. "Just How Flexible Are We?" *Library Media Connection* 26 (November 2007): 10, 12–14.

Johnson, Doug. "It's Good to Be Inflexible." *School Library Journal* 47 (November 2001): 39.

Loertscher, David V., Carol Joechlin, and Sandi Zwaan. *The New Learning Commons: Where Learners Win.* Salt Lake City, UT: Hi Willow Research and Publishing, 2009.

Markuson, Carolyn, Mary Frances Zilonis, and Mary Beth Fincke. *School Library Media Center Long-Range Planning Guide: A Workbook for Massachusetts School Library Media Centers.* bibilioTECH Corporation for the Massachusetts Board of Library Commissioners, 1999. http://www.nmrls.org/youth/school.doc.

CHAPTER 8

Budget

Every little bit of funding inches you forward toward your ideal program.

—Cynthia Anderson and Kathi Knop, *Write Grants, Get Money* (2nd ed.)

Money—if only there was an endless supply of it available to support library media programs. Jokingly, one library media specialist shared with his principal that he needed a sign to hang in the principal's office that said, "All Money Goes to the Library!" But the reality is that such a situation would be wonderful! Library media specialists look for every opportunity to increase the resources at their disposal. How does the library media specialist show that the money spent on the library is a good return on the investment? How does the library media specialist create outstanding programs on limited funds? No easy answers exist to either of these questions, but they continue to be an issue in the 21st century.

The most important thing to keep in mind is to make sure to put the learner first! How will spending these dollars help students? How will requesting that piece of equipment make an impact for student learning? What opportunities will open up for students by having this fund-raiser? Putting that in the front of one's thought process helps to create a motivation and a purpose in dealing with figuring out money and budgets.

Library Funding in the 21st Century

It has been decades since the years when school libraries were filled with federal funds. Since then, school library media centers have been in a constant battle for funding. Districts had not budgeted resources for libraries because of the federal funding, and as that dried up, there were no resources available to funnel back to libraries (Dickinson 21).

Each state (and each district and sometimes each school) set up its own ways to account for the money allocated to the library media program. Some states set specific minimums per child that must be spent, while others allow each district to determine how much money they spend. Some budgets are determined on a per pupil expenditure, while some give a flat rate to each library media center, and still others are a combination. Unfortunately in many places there is no budget for materials.

Budgeting in the 21st Century

Empowering Learners: Guidelines for School Library Media Programs (American Association of School Librarians) says that the library media programs should be sufficiently funded so that the library meets it goals, mission, priorities, and so forth. The guidelines recommend making a budget based off the long-range (or strategic) plan and meeting regularly with administrators to discuss the plan and the budget needs.

The 1960 standards recommended purchasing one book for every student each year. Almost 50 years later, that goal is very difficult for most libraries (Dickinson 86). The standards of subsequent years took out quantitative measures and focused more of qualitative measures. *Empowering Learners* is no different in that regards. The lack of specific numbers is due to the difficulty of establishing rules that will apply across the country. Each school has to set its own priorities and needs and the budget it needs to reach those. Specific standards can also be limiting. One may assume that if the minimum standard is reached then all the library media center needs have been met, when in reality they may need additional dollars because of years of neglect. This becomes another good opportunity for the library media advisory committee to weigh in on the needs of the library media program. An important conversation can be started by asking, "What does our library media program need to have to help our students be successful?"

In the 21st century, the collection has been changing. The onslaught of different formats, different pieces of technology, and so forth is having an impact on the library media budgets as well. Part of crafting the 21st-century budget will be determining what new formats need to be added to the library media center collection. Chapter 9 will focus on the collection, but it is important to mention that these new formats and resources need to be considered when creating the library media center budget.

Budget Resources

In the annual March issue of *School Library Journal* (http://www.slj.com), they usually publish the current average cost of library books. National statistics like this can be useful in determining a budget for the library. As library media specialists work to decide how many new materials they need, they can use this price to estimate the money they need to make those new purchases.

Gail Dickinson recommends using data from the local collection to determine a budget. What is the average cost of a book that the library media specialist bought last year? What was the average cost of a DVD (Dickinson 106)? She recommends doing the same with periodicals, audio/visual resources, and digital resources.

Factors to consider when making a budget are not only purchasing new materials but also including in the budget funds for replacing damaged or lost materials. Books also wear out eventually. Classics will need to be replaced from time to time. The updated covers often increase circulation of these great stories. Be prepared to replace these older books with newer copies, too.

The budget not only shows what the library media program needs but provides an outline for when funds are allocated. It shows administrators that there are specific plans for dollars that are to be spent. Library media specialists will likely have to go back to their budget to make decisions about what are priorities. If additional funding becomes available, the items eliminated from the budget can possibly still be purchased. The other thought is that they could be held over to the next year and are a starting place in creating the next budget.

Doug Johnson suggests that when working with budgets it is important to understand where your district gets its money (Johnson). Does it come from property taxes? Is it all allocated from the state? What is the budget creation process at the district level? Who makes those decisions about the budgets? Part of being prepared for budgets is researching how the process works.

Budget Justification

Do not be a library media specialist who gets a reputation for being whiny. Constantly begging "I need . . . " or "I don't have . . . " wears quickly on administrators. All the administrators hear library media specialists say is they want more money for resources, more staff, more, and more. Don't assume that they know why the library media specialist is asking for more. Everyone always wants more than what they have, but can you explain why you need it. Do not allow that perception of a whiner to establish itself. Instead, let administrators see the goals and the rationales. Provide them with the data that supports your requests. They need to know how more money and more staff will affect student achievement.

The key to any budget in a school is making it clear how those dollars are going to directly affect students and student learning. The data provided should demonstrate how the additional funding would make a difference for students. For example, when asking for additional dollars for support staff, do not focus on the library media specialist's needs and the lack of time to do administrative tasks. Do not focus on the clerical items that are not getting done. Instead, focus on the students. By having an assistant, it would free up 50 percent more of the library media specialist's time to work with students and teachers on projects. By having an assistant, books that are ordered would get in the hands of students weeks sooner. By having an assistant, the library media specialist could teach more classes in the library, in their classrooms, and in other parts of the school. By having an assistant, books that are returned could be checked in and put back on the shelves and available for the next class of students faster. This phrasing does not guarantee that the request will be granted. However, it is important to justify all expenses in terms of how they affect student learning.

Connecting the budget requests to specific curriculum projects or initiatives is important. How can the current resources of the library media center provide the tools students and teachers need? For example, with textbook adoption, the library media program could provide trade books to supplement the textbook (Cox 24). Designating part of the library media budget to fund resources to support district initiatives can be a good move both for the students and for the library media program.

More Money

Relying on dollars just from the district is not likely going to be sufficient for everything the library media program needs. Library media specialists need to be proactive to be scouting for other sources of dollars.

Grants

Grants are a great way to bring in funds to the library media center. Local educational foundations often offer annual grants for teachers in the district. These are usually simple and easy to complete. Consider writing them with a teacher in the building. The grant could also be a way to build a collaborative connection to a classroom teacher.

There are lots of other grants out there. See Figure 8.1 for just a small sample of some possible sources of grants. Make sure before applying for a grant to read the directions very carefully. Make sure the library meets the eligibility requirements of the grant. Make sure the project will meet all the grant's guidelines. Also make note of the reporting process. Finally, keep track of the deadline. Many districts require approval from the superintendent and/or school board before applying for a grant, so make sure to leave sufficient time to get their approval before the deadline. Reading all of the details of the grant is critically important in order to make good use of your grant-writing time.

Book Fairs

Book fairs have long been a source of funding for library media centers. While the library media center doesn't always receive the book fair funding, a lot of library media specialists are in charge of the fairs and therefore get to spend the profits. The money is usually kept in a building account and can be spent on a variety of things including books, magazines, videos, programs, supplies, and so forth. In some places the book fair is the library media center's sole source of funds. E-mail and Web pages have become efficient ways to promote the fair to the school and community. Communicating to the patrons the goals for which the money will be used helps to encourage people to shop at the fair. For example, the book fair might have a goal to raise money to bring an author to visit the school. Adding other family events to the evening like science fair or pizza night is another way to bring in parents to help their young ones shop.

PTA/PTOs

PTA/PTOs are another source of funding for the library media specialist. Many parent groups feel that spending money on books, technology, and programs for the media center is an excellent way to help the school. Because the library media center is a place where all students benefit from dollars spent, parent groups see that as a good place to spend their dollars. PTA/PTOs create an annual budget. With the appropriate advocacy and communications, some items for

SOURCE OF GRANT FUNDS

Parent–teacher organization.

School district educational foundation.

Library Services and Technology Act (LSTA) funds. Check with your state library to see if they have any grants for school libraries.

Corporation grants.

State and national foundations.

For more ideas, check out *Write Grants, Get Money* (2nd ed.) by Cynthia Anderson and Kathi Knop.

Figure 8.1 Grant sources.

the library media center such as an author visit or support for a reading incentive program might become annual expenses. Other things like new books, special equipment, furniture, or technology might be something that the library media specialist asks for periodically.

Wiki Wrap-Up

Money to fund programs will always be needed. Advocating for budgets that adequately fund the library media program is an annual task. However, library media specialists will need to continue to remain creative, resourceful, and inventive to find the funds to create the program students and staff deserve. For additional resources, check out the companion wiki Web site (http://www.carl-harvey.com/librarytieswiki/).

Works Cited

American Association of School Librarians. *Empowering Learners: Guidelines for School Library Media Programs.* Chicago: American Association of School Librarians, 2009.

Anderson, Cynthia and Kathi Knop. *Write Grants, Get Money* (2nd ed.). Columbus, OH: Linworth Publishing, 2009.

Cox, Marge. "Tips for Budgeting." *Library Media Connection* 26 (January 2008): 24–25.

Dickinson, Gail K. *Empty Pockets, Full Plates: Effective Budget Administration for Library Media Specialists.* Columbus, OH: Linworth Publishing, 2003.

Johnson, Doug. "Budgeting for Mean Lean Times." *Multimedia Schools* (November/December 1995). http://www.doug-johnson.com/dougwri/budgeting-for-mean-lean-times.html.

CHAPTER 9

Collections

School media centers have a unique position with a clientele that is open to a variety of new concepts and genres.

—Robyn R. Young, "Graphically Speaking: The Importance of Graphic Novels in a School Library Collection"

The elementary school library collection continues to evolve in the 21st century. The core item continues to be the book, though there are many new formats that are entering the marketplace. Determining what formats are a good investment for the school library will be an important part of developing the 21st-century library media program.

New Formats and Materials

Graphic Novel/Graphic Nonfiction

Starting in high school, this genre is expanding quickly now at the elementary level. As the popularity of graphic novels took off for older students, publishers began to take the format and apply it to books for elementary age students. There are both fiction and nonfiction graphic novels. Libraries may opt to shelve these materials where they would be found in the nonfiction or fiction section, or it may be advantageous to shelve them in a separate section so students can easily locate them.

This format also has some instructional applications. Because of the massive appeal—especially to boys—teachers and library media specialists can introduce students to writing their own stories in the graphic novel format. It could be a great exercise for writing the summary of text students have read. The graphic nonfiction book could also be a model for students to take a topic they are researching and use that format to share their findings. Software such as Comic Life is also an option for students to create a comic strip on the computer using digital pictures.

Audiobooks

There are a variety of formats for audiobooks these days. Besides the traditional cassette tape and book, now library media centers have audiobooks on compact discs, Playaways, and available for download onto mp3 players.

Playaways are not the most inexpensive format out there since they average around $30–$40 a title, but they are quickly becoming popular in elementary schools. Because they do not require a separate device to play them, it is a level playing field for all students. Students don't have to have a tape or CD player at home. They don't have to have access to those players in the classroom. They can check the Playaways out and have easy access to an audio version. Consider matching the Playaways with a copy of the book so that young readers can follow along.

Mp3 players such as iPods are also a popular format with kids of all ages. The library media center might consider a collection of them to check out to teachers to use for literacy stations. Because of the expense, it may be worthwhile to determine how they will work in the school before deciding on a procedure for students to check them out and take home. It would be important that parents are aware of the process, too, so they could help to ensure the players aren't lost or damaged.

As newer models become available, consider asking parents to donate their old iPods to the library media center. Make sure to check the licenses to see that there aren't any exclusions for libraries to purchase titles to download.

Videos

The video collections in elementary schools have been full of VHS tapes that teachers checked out to share with students as part of the instruction. Recent years have seen DVDs added to the collection as well as subscriptions to streaming video services.

Streaming video vendors include Discovery Streaming, Safari Montage, or Learn360. These online sources for videos are available from the teacher's desktop. They can be played for the entire class or set up for students to view in small groups such as at a literacy station. Some of the benefits of these streaming video services are that they provide significantly more titles than the school library could provide and, more importantly, they give the teacher the ability to pick segments and play just those parts of the video that are relevant to what students are learning.

In addition to the streaming video that is available for purchase, there are online video sources that are free. The most widely known, of course, is YouTube (http://www.youtube.com). It is also one of the most blocked Web sites in schools. YouTube has created a more school friendly version—TeacherTube (http://www.teachertube.com). It is possible that school districts may be more inclined to unblock TeacherTube to gain access to some of the rich video content posted there. As with all content, it is important to preview the material before using it with students.

However, as with all video content, it is important to preview and watch it in its entirety before sharing it with students. Surprises are never fun when they show up on the TV screen, so to avoid anything that might not be appropriate it is best to always watch the entire clip first. Because TeacherTube is also a creation of videos posted by others, it is important when choosing videos to share with students that one also makes sure to validate that they are accurate and that they follow copyright guidelines for use of images and sounds.

Online Resources

Chapter 6 covered various online resources including online databases, Web sites, and Web 2.0 tools. However, one other online format that was not mentioned in Chapter 6 applies more appropriately to the collection development chapter. Several companies are bringing children's books to life via online videos. Companies such as Scholastic's Book Flix or Tumblebooks are available for an annual subscription fee. Depending on the license, these online tools can also be used at home. They are very popular resources for literacy stations in elementary schools, too.

Professional Collections

Professional resources are also an important part of any collection. The professional collection should contain resources that teachers want and need to stay current in what are the best practices in education.

Besides the traditional print collection of books and magazines, consider online options as well. The library media specialist could create a wiki based on the school improvement goals. As there are online articles, blog entries, and so forth, the library media specialist could post links of interest to the wiki for the rest of the staff to read. Because the site is a wiki, anyone on the staff could add to it as well, building an even stronger collection for everyone. It could even be as specific as a list of what professional resources would be helpful to specific grade levels based on the discussions in their professional learning communities.

In addition, the library media specialist should make sure to include titles from publishers such as Linworth or Libraries Unlimited in the professional collection that will help them grow and develop professionally as well. Library media specialists should also have access to periodicals such as *Library Media Connection, School Library Journal,* and *School Library Media Activities Monthly.* Library media specialists in a district might consider pooling their resources to share books and magazine subscriptions.

Just as with the teacher resources, relying strictly on print is limiting to the discussion. In Chapter 11, there will be discussion about creating a Personal Learning Network as well as connecting to library media professionals all over the world with blogs, Twitter, and so forth. However, while we're in the collection development chapter, it is important to mention that there is a huge network of bloggers focused on children's literature. The KidLitosphere, as it is called, includes bloggers from librarians to teachers to authors to publishers who are all sharing their thoughts, ideas, favorite new books, and so forth (http://kidlitosphere.org/Kid Litosphere_Central/Welcome.html). They have compiled many of the best bloggers for one to consider reading.

Other Collections
Leveled Library Resources

Leveled libraries are huge parts of the resources available in elementary schools. These collections contain multiple copies of books grouped together by levels. Looking at these libraries as an opportunity, the library media specialist can help select, organize, catalog, and manage the leveled library. Automation systems can track data about the use of the materials in that room. Library media specialists can make sure to track all the resources funneled into the leveled library. By being part of the solution in helping create these leveled libraries, library media specialists can demonstrate how that room serves a purpose different than that of the library media center. Library media centers need to remain free choice and unleveled, and by being part of the solution of creating a leveled library, library media specialists can help keep it that way (Harvey "Leveling").

Textbooks

Textbooks are another resource that will see dramatic change during the 21st century. Currently the print model dominates, but publishers are offering more and more options for electronic textbooks for students. Whether the book is on a CD, online, or in a print volume, automation systems can also help districts track their textbooks. Destiny by Follett, for example, has a complete module designed to help districts track textbooks. While this may seem like something the library media specialist should avoid because it is just one more thing to do, keep in mind that library media specialists are the experts in keeping track of resources. There is some logic in the thought that they would be part of keeping track of textbooks as well. Being part of the solution can be important when it comes to the library media program needing things, too (Harvey "Textbooks").

Equipment and/or Technology

As discussed in Chapters 6 and 8, equipment and technology purchases are not always something at the discretion of the library media specialist. However, it is important that the library media specialist be aware of what types of resources are out there and be ready to offer advice and advocate for those resources a school library (and the entire school) needs to have.

Weeding

Weeding the collection is vitally important. Outdated and worn materials make the library unappealing to students. In addition, they can be filled with misinformation. Take time to set up a system to periodically weed the collection to eliminate those resources that are old and outdated. Make sure to follow district policies for discarding the weeded materials.

One method commonly used in libraries is the Continuous Review, Evaluation, and Weeding (CREW) method. The Texas State Library publishes these guidelines and methods for weeding the collection (www.tsl.state.tx.us/ld/pubs/crew/). Heinemann/Raintree Publishers have also taken over a service originally started by SUNLINK in Florida that provides a weed of the month topic (http://www.heinemannlibrary.com/weed/index.asp). These monthly recommendations of areas of the collection to weed are a good way to keep the collection weeded at a reasonable pace rather than doing it all at once.

It is also important to review and weed our virtual library media centers. Links and resources change constantly, so it is important to check the links on the library media center Web site as well. Remove those sites that have gone defunct and add new ones to support specific projects and activities.

Wiki Wrap-Up

Collection development in the 21st century will require library media specialists to think about the new formats and new sources students will need to find information. Appendix A contains a list of some of the most common library media vendors. These resources provided by the library media program for students and staff will be important to prepare them for the 21st century. For additional resources, check out the companion wiki Web site (http://www.carl-harvey. com/librarytieswiki/).

Works Cited

Harvey, Carl A., II. "Leveling for Leverage." *Library Media Connection* 24 (January 2006): 42–43.

Harvey, Carl A., II. "Textbooks: Friend or Foe." *Library Media Connection* 26 (January 2008): 52–53.

CHAPTER 10

Advocacy, Public Relations, and Marketing

Too many administrators are still wondering what library media specialist do besides check out books.

—Mary Alice Anderson, "Leadership: What Makes Us Tick?"

Defining Advocacy, Public Relations, and Marketing

Because of the loss of positions and cuts in library budgets, it has become even more urgent for library media specialists to work on public relations and advocacy. Advocacy efforts often begin too late. Once it is announced that positions may be cut or eliminated, often there is little to be done to save them. The work with public relations and advocacy must become a constant part of the library media program.

Advocacy is when someone other than the library media specialist shares the message and fights for the library media program (American Association of School Librarians [AASL]). Advocacy entails getting parents, students, staff, and community members to know and understand the importance of the library media program and to be willing to go to bat for it. These are the people who school boards and administrators will listen to when making decisions. When library media specialists speak, it often is seen as self-serving, but when a parent talks about the value of the program, they are perceived as speaking with sincerity and a real-life story.

Public relations includes all the work the library media specialist does to share what is happening in the library media center, why it is important, and how it connects to the curriculum. This communication is one-way—from the library media specialist to the stakeholders (AASL).

This can be done via newsletters, e-mails, face-to-face conversations, students sharing at home what they did at school that day, articles in the newspaper, and so forth. In the 21st century, tools like blogs and wikis are ways to share with parents and students the happenings in the library media center.

Marketing involves developing a plan of what customers need and how the library media program can provide those services (AASL). This dovetails perfectly into the long-range plans discussed in Chapter 7. The library media specialist uses public relations to promote the services outlined in the plan and then when patrons are getting the services they need they in turn become advocates for the library media center!

Advocates

School libraries are often first on the list to be eliminated during tough financial times. Once the positions are gone, it is difficult to get them back. By building advocates, the library media specialist creates a group of people who are willing to go to bat in those difficult times to say that eliminating or cutting school libraries is not the answer to the budget problems. Building advocacy creates a network of people who are sharing what is happening in the library media program out in the community so that maybe the discussion of cuts will never come up.

Building Advocates

Creating advocates for the library media center is about building partnerships. Partnerships with principals, parents, and students are crucial so that they see why the library media center is so important. For administrators it might be how the library media program plays a critical role in achieving the school improvement goals. For parents it might be how the library media program provides critical resources and support for helping their child learn to read and for developing lifelong learners. For students it might be the support they receive from the library media specialist during a research project or guidance on finding the perfect book. Connecting the goals of the library media program to the goals of the stakeholders is the link that helps to building advocates.

Do not expect that just by doing the job (and doing it well), advocates will instantly appear. Doing a great job is only the first step. Creating advocates also requires educating them on why the library media program is critical. They need to see examples. Show them:

✦ How the library media program contributes to the school improvement plan.

✦ How the library media program circulation statistics show a connection to improving students' reading skills.

✦ How what happens in the library media center affects standardized test scores.

✦ How the collaboration log demonstrates that the 21st-century skills are embedded into instruction.

Never assume that someone "gets it" by just watching. Take time to talk with the advocates and show them the data proving that the library media program is a critical element in the school.

Promotion

Library media specialists tend to be quiet. No, not that stereotypical shusher; rather, they do not tend to share the great things happening in their library media center. Library media specialists need to be telling the story of what is happening in the library media program. Share the great student accomplishments and how they are important to the school.

Some adults have no memory of an elementary library media center. Some schools might have just had a few shelves in the back of the classroom that every nine weeks the custodians rotated among the four elementary buildings so there was a new selection of books to choose from. A lot of the books were from the 50s, 60s, and 70s and had been rebound at least once. Others may remember the cranky old lady who quickly checked out the books to the students to get them out of the library. She may have been called the librarian even if she wasn't a trained professional. If those are all the memories someone has about the library media center, how can he ever begin to conceptualize its importance? The answer can be simple. The library media specialist needs to paint a new positive image for him of what the library can do.

This is a very common situation for library media programs. While there has been a huge evolution in what the library media programs do and the role the library media specialist plays, the perception some people have of school libraries has not changed. The library media specialist needs to be in the forefront, showing people the library media program of the 21st century.

Some may think that promoting the library media program takes up valuable time when they could be working with students or teachers, but the time is well spent when those students, teachers, and administrators really begin to understand what the library media program is all about.

Designing Promotions

Chapter 3 provided a plethora of resources to use to communicate with stakeholders. Take advantage of those communication vehicles. They can be very powerful in sharing the message about the library media center. In reality, almost anything the library media specialist does can be an opportunity to promote the library media program.

Invite teachers down to see the new resources that have just arrived. Mingle among them and point out books that might be helpful to them. Talk about ideas of possible projects based on the books. Following the teacher preview, leave the books out so students can begin checking them out. Highlight some of the new formats of materials at a staff meeting. Share a new online tool periodically. Introduce the tool at a staff meeting, follow up with e-mail, and then visit their professional learning community (PLC) time to offer individual support.

Bringing authors to schools is an exciting way to engage students in the love of reading and writing. It creates a memory for them they will have with them long after they leave the doors of the school. When inviting an author to visit the school, put together a simple invitation. Send it to every central office administrator and the school board members. This gives them a glimpse into the special events happening in the library media center. In addition, library media specialists collaborate each year to create a packet of projects and resources to share with the teachers about the visiting author. The packet shows them how it connects to what they are teaching in the classroom. Invite parents to come and see the author presentations, because while an author visit might just be a one-time deal, if the students, teachers, and parents get excited about the event, the PTO just might set up an annual line item in their budget.

Invite administrators to the library media center so they can see the work students are doing. Encourage them to talk to students about what they are working on. Highlight projects in the library media center newsletter and blog so that teachers can be recognized for collaborating with the library media specialist. Take pictures of events, lessons, projects, speakers, and so forth. These can be used in newsletters, on the Web, parts of presentations, blogs, and so forth. Have students record a week in review podcast that students and parents can listen to over the Internet.

Simple statistics about the library can turn into public relations elements, too. For example, one library media specialist added up all the grants he had received in the past five years. Some of these directly benefited the library and others were written to help resources in the school such as the leveled library. When the tally was done, it added up to over $50,000, so the library media specialist sent off a quick e-mail to the principal. The principal was so impressed that he put in the next school newsletter how much money had been raised because of the library media program.

Marketing Plan

Marketing the media center program goes hand in hand with the long-range plans discussed in Chapter 7. Another element of long-rang planning is doing research to determine the needs of the users. This is a critical step in long-range planning. While the library media program is based on what students need to learn, at the same time it needs to be responsive to the recreational needs of student as well. The formats of materials, the types of resources, the types of recreational reading, the layout of the facility, and so forth are all elements that can control how inviting the media center is and how much the user comes to the library media center. It is another data point that will be helpful in designing a long-range plan to move the library forward.

Resources

The AASL provides a wealth of resources to support advocacy efforts at the local level. The Advocacy Toolkit (http://www.ala.org/ala/mgrps/divs/aasl/aaslissues/toolkits/aasladvocacy.cfm) provides resources to develop a public awareness campaign for your school library media center. The School Library Health and Wellness Toolkit (http://www.ala.org/ala/mgrps/divs/aasl/aaslissues/toolkits/slmhealthandwellness.cfm) is designed to help library media specialists be proactive in garnering supporters for the school library. The time to be prepared is long before any cuts are considered. The final kit provides resources for when the budget ax is just about to fall. The Crisis Toolkit (http://www.ala.org/ala/mgrps/divs/aasl/aaslissues/toolkits/crisis.cfm) is there to help when positions or budgets are being cut.

Wiki Wrap-Up

Advocates promote and support library media programs. Every program needs to ensure it has a strong contingency of advocates who are there in times of good and bad. Waiting until the damage is done is too late. Advocacy requires people to be proactive! Success will have been achieved when no one would even think of eliminating or cutting school library media programs. For additional resources, check out the companion wiki Web site (http://www.carl-harvey.com/librarytieswiki/).

Works Cited

American Association of School Librarians. "Definitions of Advocacy, PR, Marketing." May 9, 2009, http://www.ala.org/ala/mgrps/divs/aasl/aaslissues/aasladvocacy/definitions.cfm.

Anderson, Mary Alice. "Leadership: What Makes Us Tick?" *Library Media Connection* 24 (March 2006): 15–19.

CHAPTER 11

Leadership

Opportunities for leadership for the library media specialist are many. Library media specialists have to take the initiative when it comes to becoming a leader in their school and in school improvement, because those will be critical elements in creating successful and thriving library media programs.

—Carl A. Harvey II, *No School Library Left Behind: Leadership, School Improvement, and the Media Specialist*

Allison Zmuda and Violet Harada, in their book *Librarians as Learning Specialists,* argue that library media specialists have to take responsibility for the learning that happens in the library media center and demand that the quality of instruction meets high standards. Teachers often want to come in to do a very low-level fact and find project. Library media specialists have to be willing to help that teacher see other opportunities that would be more meaningful for the students. Library media specialists have to move beyond just the perception of that person who deals with books and instead be seen as a curriculum leader with a wealth of resources and ideas ready to implement.

Library media specialists have to reach beyond the library and be active participants in the school, which in turn will help the library media program grow. Volunteer to serve on building committees such as the influential school improvement committee. Be aware of new initiatives and school-wide campaigns, and then articulate how the library media program can support and enhance those initiatives. Recently on a listserv, a library media specialist posted about a new initiative happening in the school, and he wondered if any library media specialists had been a part of it. Several of the replies said they had tried to stay clear of the curricular initiative, as they didn't see how it affected the library media program. Taking a head-in-the-sand approach leaves the library media program out of the loop. The library media program has the potential to be a great influence on almost any initiative in the school. It is important to take the lead and be part of the conversation.

Consider the school that was designing a new behavior plan model. The emotional disability teacher was leading the planning and was given a release day to work on it. She asked the library media specialist to help because she knew he had a global perspective of the school, access to finding resources, and technology skills. Strong advocacy for the program and consistent collaboration with colleagues will build opportunities for the library media specialist to influence what happens in the school.

The library media profession can be one of isolation. Often schools are staffed with only one library media specialist, so there is no one else who can relate to the job the library media specialist does. Professional organizations and resources provide connections to those who understand. Networking with colleagues face-to-face at conferences and virtually through tools like LM_Net, Teacher Librarian Ning, blogs, and so forth all are an important part of how the library media specialist can connect with others and grow. The old adages of "I don't have time to learn about a _____ (blog, ning, wiki, listserv, etc.)" or "I can't be away from my library" are positions that are contrary to professional growth. The reality is that a library media specialist cannot be successful in the 21st century without building these contacts and using these tools. Library media specialists need to be life-long learners just like the students!

Library Media Specialist
Professional Organizations

Long ago it was just an expectation that everyone joined the professional organization associated with his or her career. In today's world, that does not seem to be the case. If one is around the American Association of School Librarians (AASL) Affiliate Assembly, they often hear that many state organizations have seen a decline in membership in recent years. However, library media specialists who do not belong to their state and national organization have no idea what they are missing. Professional organizations should be a part of any personal learning network. The resources, the networking, the advocacy, the conferences, and the sense of belonging are essential to creating a 21st-century library media center.

It is not cheap to belong to a professional organization, but one has to be a member to have a voice in the organization. Even if one can't attend the conferences, there are still opportunities for virtual participation on committees. Library media specialists don't have the right to complain about what their state or national organization does or doesn't do if they aren't members. They have the opportunity to voice their opinions and thoughts as members. Many organizations are also beginning to tap into these online tools such as blogs, wikis, and so forth to connect with people all over the state and country.

Professional organizations are advocating for library media specialists, so the more members the organization has, the stronger its voice becomes. The contacts that one makes through a professional organization become a network of colleagues to call on when advice and counsel are needed. When attending a national (or state) conference for the first time, one gets the opportunities to listen and meet those people who are leading the profession. Not only are they just ordinary people, but they want to learn just as much from you as you want to learn from them, which makes the experience a two-way learning adventure.

AASL, for example, has released new major standards for student learning, a guide for putting those standards into action, and new program guidelines in the last couple of years. These are major undertakings that the professional organization does for the entire library community. Being a member helps to support the organization that is leading in defining what our profession will look like in the years ahead.

Finally, there is much to be said for giving back to a profession. It is important to belong, to be an active member, to serve on committees, and so forth. Being active in the profession gives one the ability to help make the profession even better. Each year when the renewal form for membership arrives in the mailbox (or e-mail inbox), think about how belonging helps improve library media centers across the state and country. Don't miss out on a minute of the opportunities that lie ahead in the coming year. So join now!

Professional Development

The traditional forms of professional development such as conferences, workshops, and classes are all available and certainly viable opportunities for learning.

AASL hosts a national conference every two years and a national institute on the off-conference years. The largest national library conferences are the American Library Association's (ALA) annual conference and midwinter meetings. These two events each year are where the heart of the work for the national professional organization is done.

Beyond ALA and AASL, there are also other national conferences that may appeal to school librarians. The International Society for Technology in Education's (ISTE) annual conference each summer is packed full of technology resources and uses in education. ISTE's Special Interest Group for Media Specialists (SIGMS) is growing every year and presenting a large presence at the conference. The only conflict is that the NECC and ALA annual conference often overlap, making it difficult for those who would like to attend both conferences.

The International Reading Association's (IRA) annual conference also provides another opportunity for library media specialists as it connects with the mission to develop life-long readers. IRA also holds regional conferences. Because of the variety of roles library media specialists play, there are many conferences and professional opportunities that will develop skills, build networks, and become innovators and leaders. Choosing which conferences to attend and which sessions at the conference to participate in can become the hard part.

Most state library associations have their own conference each year. This is a good place for hearing what others in the state are doing. In addition, they are a good place for the library media specialist to share some of the good things happening in his or her library. The connection with vendors at conferences is also a great time to get up to speed on what new tools and resources are available.

However, there are other ways to connect for professional development beyond just face-to-face conferences. David Warlick describes creating a personal learning network or PLN (Warlick).

This network provides daily opportunities for learning and sharing ideas. He has an inspiration web on his Web site (http://landmark-project.com/workshops/personallearningnetwork.htm) that gives a visual perspective to this idea of a PLN. There are lots of opportunities for the library media specialist to build his or her own PLN, too.

LM_Net (http://www.eduref.org/lm_net/) has been around since the early 1990s and is one of the most active listservs in the country. Every library media specialist should join and become one of the 10,000-plus members. It is a forum for sharing and learning together. As Web 2.0 technology, LM_Net has taken off in new directions with its own LM_Net wiki (http://lmnet. wikispaces.com), where documents, presentations, and other resources that don't work over e-mail can be posted for all to share.

Joyce Valenza started another forum for library media specialists to interact with each other—the Teacher-Librarian Ning. The ning devoted to school libraries (http://teacherlibrarian.ning.com) boasts over 1,800 members. This social network has lots of forums and groups that people can use to share and learn from each other.

There are lots of tools that can be use to expand one's personal learning network as well, such as blogs, Twitter, Second Life, Facebook, and so forth. All of these are places where library media specialists can gather, interact with other library media specialists (and other educators), and continue to learn and expand their knowledge of this changing information landscape.

Webinars are also a new popular format for professional development. Linworth Publishing has been offering a Webinar series each semester for the last year or so. AASL just completed a Webinar series about the new standards. The ability to attend a workshop without leaving the confines of the library or your house can be appealing.

Something else to ponder is staff development that happens in the school. Often, library media specialists are left out of the loop on some of these trainings because the person planning may think it does not apply to the library media specialist. However, library media specialists should be part of those trainings. Consider the example of a building that opted to implement the Dynamic Indicators of Basic Early Literacy Skills (DIBELS) as one form of assessment. DIBELS is a set of tests given three times a year. Each one is less than a minute and gives quick feedback on students' literacy development. Students who need additional support are retested periodically between the three benchmark tests to determine if interventions are begin successful. As with most things, there are those who like DIBELS and those that don't. Now, putting aside opinions about DIBELS, this was going to be a school-wide initiative, so the library media specialist felt it was important to attend. It was never intended that the library media specialist would give DIBELS tests, but knowing what the tests were and how they were administered could be helpful in analyzing the data and when collaborating with teachers.

Writing and Presenting

Often, the first response when someone suggests to a library media specialist to write an article or turn in a proposal to present at a conference is "I don't do anything that special" or "I don't have time for that." Library media specialists are way too modest. Sharing the great things ones does is not only helpful to other library media specialists but is a major learning opportunity for the library media specialist as well.

Writing an article or giving a presentation is a very reflective experience. It gives the library media specialist the chance to sit back and think about the project—what went well, what could go better the next time, what did the students learn, and so forth. Reflection is a critical part of the learning process, and often one does not take time to do it because as soon as one project is finished the next one is starting. When one writes or presents, it forces one to make time to reflect and rethink the entire project.

Another reflective opportunity is to post periodically on a blog. The element that is added here is the ability to interact with the readers. People can comment on the reflection for a dialogue to be created and thereby improve on the project even more. Sharing provides an avenue to bring one outside of library media centers and reflect on making the library media program even better. Remember that the blog is out there for all to read, so make sure that as one writes about one's experience that one makes sure it is something that one wouldn't mind one's principal or superintendent to read.

Building/District Leadership
Professional Development

Library media specialists should be an active part of providing professional development in their buildings. They work with every teacher in the building. They are natural leaders in using technology in the building. They hold a bounty of resources in the library media centers. Combine all this together and it makes logical sense that library media specialists should be offering professional development to teachers.

The strength in library media programs comes from both literacy and technology. The library media specialist has on her agenda to help teachers use technology effectively and give teachers ideas for helping their students with reading, research, writing, and so forth. Before starting, make sure to assess the staff with a survey or other instrument to determine what their needs really are. If they all know what a blog is, then one could skip the introductory lesson. The survey also needs to take into account the school improvement goals. Any professional development that is offered should connect back to that plan.

Make sure you market your session by offering a title that applies to the school improvement plans and sounds inviting. Title the session "Using Digital Video Cameras as a Literacy Station" or "Using Digital Video Cameras as a Fluency Monitor" and teachers will be interested in attending and engaged in the session. For example, one library media specialist knew the focus of the building was on literacy stations. So, each month he offered a short, 30-minute session focusing on one piece of technology and how it connected to literacy stations.

Using technology as a training tool is also important. Library media specialists should model best practices. Put handouts for the workshops up on the library media center wiki. Also include on the wiki things like a weekly Web site for teachers. It gives the library media specialist just one more way to share ideas and offer suggestions and to be seen as a leader.

Another library media specialist used a Moodle server to organize a staff book study over the summer. Teachers could log in and participate on their own time. Modeling these tools and resources when working with teachers provides a glimpse of the potential with students. This can sometimes be the most powerful professional development the library media specialist can offer.

Committees

Everybody wishes they could attend more meetings—OK, maybe not. But, the library media specialist has an important voice that needs to be heard. When the opportunity to serve on district committees comes along, one should consider volunteering for it. Technology, English language learners, school improvement, textbook adoption, or whatever the committee might be all have a purpose in helping the district move forward. Having a library media specialist on these committees provides a perspective that is important, and it is key for people to see the library media specialist as helping to work toward solutions.

The same applies for building-level committees, too. Look at the committees that the library media program can best be of assistance to, such as a literacy or technology committee. In addition, be involved in those committees that make important decisions, such as a data analysis or school improvement team. Being active and involved in the building, in the district, and in the professional organizations will only help one be a better library media specialist.

Wiki Wrap-Up

Twenty-first-century library media specialists are leaders! Developing leadership skills is a critical component to the job. Library media specialists need to help to lead and guide the building, the district, and the profession. As leaders in the 21st century, library media specialists have great potential. They have great potential for affecting student achievement. They have great potential to affect curriculum. They can have great potential to affect professional development. They have great potential to change the perceptions of school library media programs. Those are some great opportunities in the 21st century. Now library media specialists need to just take advantage of them! For additional resources, check out the companion wiki Web site (http://www.carl-harvey.com/librarytieswiki/).

Works Cited

Warlick, David. "The Art and Technique of Personal Learning Networks." *David Warlick's CoLearners Wiki*. August 31, 2008, http://davidwarlick.com/wiki/pmwiki.php/main/theartamptechniqueofcultivatingyourpersonallearningnetwork.

Zmuda, Allison and Violet H. Harada. *Librarians as Learning Specialists: Meeting the Learning Imperative for the 21st Century.* Westport, CT: Libraries Unlimited, 2008.

APPENDIX A

Audio Resources

Books on Tape: http://www.booksontape.com *

Library Video Company: http://www.libraryvideo.com

Overdrive School Download Library: http://www.overdrive.com

Recorded Books: http://www.recordedbooks.com *

Video Resources

Discovery Education: http://streaming.discoveryeducation.com

Disney Educational Products: http://dep.disney.go.com

Library Video Company: http://www.libraryvideo.com

Safari Montage: http://www.safarimontage.com

Spoken Arts Media: http://www.spokenartsmedia.com/home.htm

Weston Woods: http://teacher.scholastic.com/products/westonwoods

Book Publishers

ABDO Publishing Group: http://www.abdopublishing.com

Bearport Publishing Company: http://www.bearportpublishing.com

---

*Indicates Web site has a blog or RSS feed.

Benchmark Books (Marshall Cavendish): http://www.marshallcavendish.us

Capstone Publishers: http://www.coughlan-companies.com

Chelsea Clubhouse (Chelsea House): http://chelseahouse.infobasepublishing.com

Crabtree Publishing: http://www.crabtreebooks.com

DK Publishing: http://us.dk.com

Enslow Publishers: http://www.enslow.com

Gareth Stevens Publishing: http://www.garethstevens.com

Heinemann Library/Raintree: http://www.heinemannlibrary.com

Lerner Publishing Group: http://www.lernerbooks.com

Norwood House Press: http://www.norwoodhousepress.com

Rosen Publishing: http://www.rosenpublishing.com

Rourke Publishing: http://www.rourkepublishing.com

Scholastic: http://www.scholastic.com

Scholastic Library Publishing: http://www.scholastic.com/librarypublishing

Weigl Publishers: http://www.weigl.com/american.asp

World Book: http://www.worldbook.com

Graphic Novels/Nonfiction

First Second (Roaring Brook Press) http://firstsecondbooks.typepad.com *

Stone Arch Books: http://www.stonearchbooks.com *

Toon Books: http://www.toon-books.com *

UDON Entertainment: http://www.udonentertainment.com/blog/ *

Databases

Capstone Publishing: http://www.coughlan-companies.com

EBSCO: http://www.ebsco.com

Gale—Cengage Learning: http://www.gale.cengage.com

Grolier Online/Book Flix: http://www.scholastic.com

ProQuest: http://www.il.proquest.com

TeachingBooks.net: http://www.teachingbooks.net *

World Book Online: http://www.worldbookonline.com

Jobbers

Baker & Taylor: http://www.btol.com

Bound to Stay Bound Books: http://www.btsb.com

Follett Library Resource: http://www.flr.com

Mackin Library Media: http://www.mackin.com

Perma-Bound: http://www.perma-bound.com

Rainbow Book Company: http://www.rainbowbookcompany.com

Periodicals

EBSCO Information Services: http://www.ebsco.com

Library Media Connection: http://www.librarymediaconnection.com

School Library Journal: http://www.slj.com *

School Library Monthly: http://www.schoollibrarymonthly.com *

Teacher-Librarian Magazine: http://www.teacher-librarian.com

Professional Materials

American Library Association Editions: http://alastore.ala.org *

Libraries Unlimited: http://www.lu.com

Linworth Publishing: http://www.linworth.com

Neal-Schuman Publishers: http://www.neal-schuman.com *

Supplies

Brodart: http://www.brodart.com

DEMCO: http://www.demco.com

Highsmith: http://www.highsmith.com

APPENDIX B

Library Media/ Technology Personal Learning Network

Library Media/Tech Leaders Blogs

- ✦ American Association of School Librarians Blog

    http://www.aasl.ala.org/aaslblog/

- ✦ Diane Chen's Practically Paradise

    http://www.schoollibraryjournal.com/blog/830000283.html?nid=3368

- ✦ Christopher Harris's Infomancy

    http://schoolof.info/infomancy/

- ✦ Frances Harris's Gargoyles Loose in the Library

    http://www.uni.uiuc.edu/library/blog/

- ✦ Carl Harvey's Library Ties

    http://www.carl-harvey.com/libraryties/

- ✦ Jacquie Henry's Wanderings . . .

    http://wanderings.edublogs.org/

- ✦ Kevin Jarrett's Welcome to NCS-Tech!

    http://www.ncs-tech.org

- ✦ Doug Johnson's Blue Skunk Blog

    http://doug-johnson.squarespace.com/blue-skunk-blog/

- ✦ Cathy Nelson's Professional Thoughts

    http://blog.cathyjonelson.com/

- ✦ Judy O'Connell's HeyJude

    http://heyjude.wordpress.com

- ✦ Floyd Pentlin's School Libraries: The Steak and the Sizzle

    http://fpentlin.edublogs.org/

- ✦ Will Richardson's Weblogg-ed

    http://weblogg-ed.com

- ✦ School Library Monthly (Moderated by Kristin Fontichiaro)

    http://blog.schoollibrarymonthly.com

- ✦ Kathy Schrock's Kaffeeklatsch

    http://kathyschrock.net/blog/index.htm

- ✦ School Library Media Activities Monthly Blog—Kristin Fontichiaro

    http://blog.schoollibrarymedia.com/

- ✦ Joyce Valenza's Never Ending Search Blog

    http://www.schoollibraryjournal.com/blog/1340000334.html?nid=3714

- ✦ David Warlick's 2¢ Worth

    http://davidwarlick.com/2cents

- ✦ Alice Yucht's Alice in InfoLand

    http://www.aliceinfo.org/blog/

Library Media/Tech Leaders Wikis

- ✦ Carl Harvey's 21st Century Elementary Library Program

    http://www.carl-harvey.com/librarytieswiki/

- ✦ Doug Johnson

    http://dougjohnson.wikispaces.com/

- ✦ David Loertscher's Professional Reviews

    http://professionalreviews.pbwiki.com/

- ✦ Joyce Valenza's Information Fluency

    http://informationfluency.wikispaces.com/

- ✦ Alice Yucht

    http://aliceyucht.pbworks.com

Library Media/Tech Leaders on Twitter

- ✦ AASL (aasl)
- ✦ ALA Library (alalibrary)

- ✦ ALA News (alanews)
- ✦ The Big6 (thebig6)
- ✦ Carolyn Foote (technolibrary)
- ✦ Carl Harvey (caharvey2)
- ✦ Kevin Jarrett (kjarrett)
- ✦ Cathy Nelson (cathyjo)
- ✦ Judy O'Connell (heyjudeonline)
- ✦ Will Richardson (willrich45)
- ✦ School Library Journal (sljournal)
- ✦ Kathy Schrock (kathyschrock)
- ✦ TeachingBooks.net (TeachingBooks)
- ✦ Joyce Valenza (joycevalenza)
- ✦ David Warlick (dwarlick)
- ✦ Alice Yucht (ayucht)
- ✦ Another source to find library media specialists on Twitter:

  http://twitter4teachers.pbworks.com/Librarians

Library Media/Tech Social Networking

Facebook—http://www.facebook.com

There are many library media specialists on Facebook. Remember that they will have to decide whether to accept any friend requests. There are also many library-related groups such as AASL, ALA, *School Library Journal,* and ISTE.

LinkedIn—http://www.linkedin.com

This is another social network specifically targeted at professionals from all types of professions and all around the world. There are also library-related groups in LinkedIn as well.

Second Life—http://secondlife.com

There are many library media specialist on Second Life. ISTE's Special Interest Group for Media Specialist (sigms) have been hosting programming for library media specialist. Working in collaboration with AASL, these event shave helped orient library media specialists to the virtual reality environment and provided a forum for networking and collaboration. Check out the sigms wiki for more information: http://sigms.iste.wikispaces.net/SIGMS+in+Second+Life.

Teacher-Librarian Ning – http://teacherlibrarian.ning.com

The Teacher-Librarian Ning is another social network vehicle where library media specialists can share and collaborate with each other. Started by Joyce Valenza, this is a growing community.

Library Media/Tech Listservs

LM_Net: to subscribe, go to http://www.eduref.org/lm_net/

AASL Forum: to subscribe, go to http://www.ala.org/ala/mgrps/divs/aasl/aboutaasl/aaslcommunity/communityinaasl/aasledisclist/aaslforum.cfm

APPENDIX C

Web 2.0 Examples

Blogs

Grandview Elementary School

http://www.grandviewlibrary.org/StudentBlogs.aspx

Willowdale Elementary

http://www.mpsomaha.org/willow/blog/index.html

Marin County Day School's Blogs

http://mcdsblogs.org/

Sope Creek Elementary Library Media Center

http://sopecreeklibrary.typepad.com/

Jesse Boyd Elementary Library Blog

http://spart7.info/boydblog

Northside Elementary Library—Book Blog

http://ilearn.woodfordschools.org/shorowitz

North Elementary School Library Media Center

http://northlmc.wikispaces.com

The Blogging Libraries Wiki (list of school library blogs)

http://www.blogwithoutalibrary.net/links/index.php?title=School_libraries

Wikis

Activity Starters from Annette Lamb

http://readwritewiki.wikispaces.com

Willowdale Elementary School

http://www.mpsomaha.org/willow/Radio/

Jamestown Elementary School

http://slapcast.com/users/Jamestown

E.R. Andrews Elementary School

http://erandrewslibrary.pbworks.com

Village Elementary School

http://villagewiki.pbworks.com/FrontPage

Podcasts

Beverly Elementary School

http://www.birmingham.k12.mi.us/Schools/Elementary/Beverly/Media+Center/Podcasts.htm

Branson Elementary Library Media Center

http://www.branson.k12.mo.us/elementary/podcast/

Pittsford Central Schools

http://www.pittsfordschools.org/podcasts.cfm

Education Podcast Network

http://epnweb.org/index.php?openpod=16

Willow Elementary School

http://www.mpsomaha.org/willow/Radio/

Cambridge Elementary School

http://www.ahisd.net/campuses/Cambridge/radio/radio.htm

Index